THE LAST TEAR

REACHING TO INFINITE LOVE

By Simran Khan

First Published in 2021

Becomeshakespeare.com

One Point Six Technologies Pvt Ltd
123, Building J2, Shram Seva Premises,
Wadala Truck Depot, Wadala (East),
Mumbai 400037, India
T: +91 8080226699

ISBN - 978-93-5438-551-3

About the Author

Author is a social scientist. Her work across multiple disciplines broadly addresses narratives of human experiences . Being a social scientist Simran also worked as a faculty member in the field of History and Political science.

In her other life she is an MBA graduate and to explore human behaviour more she is now pursuing a degree in psychology.

She's being into writing since she was in grade 7. Her talent of writing was recognised when her poem got featured in her school's magazine same year.

Apart from this she shares her interest in painting, dancing and crooning.

Acknowledgment

No matter what you achieve, or whichever project you are working on, though you may be working alone and physically it looks like this.

But behind the curtains, someone may have motivated you, someone may have given you constructive criticism. Someone's wise advice may have worked as life saviour for your project.

Thus..its 'Us' in the picture and 'We did it'.

For the same- Thank you Almighty, Maa Paa, siblings, Ravi bhaiya, Vansh, Devanshi and Arshiya.

Chapter 1
The mystery around her

"Who is she? Where has she come from?" asked Anjali, a tall, statuesque woman who worked as a nurse in the Kalyani Hospital.

"I have no idea" replied Rauf, a compounder. "A man brought her here. He said she was lying on the road. Perhaps, it's a hit and run case" he added while carrying the stretcher to the emergency ward.

Kalyani Hospital was a life saviour for many people. Serving from last 20 years with a philanthropic desire to assuage the sufferings of the destitute, it was a tall, imposing structure that stood on a vast area, and had a compassionate and proficient workforce.

The staff and the patient reached the ward. Dr Sinha, a senior doctor, delicately held the lady's wrist. After going through an array of their medical proficiencies, the team of saviours could finally breathe a sigh of relief when the lady's condition shifted to a safe zone.

"Okay...her condition is stable now, but she is not ready to be shifted to the general ward. Nurse, take care of her; call me when she is conscious" instructed Dr Sinha.

"Yes sir" replied Anjali.

At the main gate of the hospital a light brown coloured police jeep came to a screeching halt. A tall, broad-shouldered man with a heroic personality stepped out of the vehicle and entered the hospital. He headed towards the receptionist and said "Hello miss, can you please tell me where the hit and run case victim has been kept?"

"Yes sir. She is in the emergency ward, bed no. 8."

"Thank you, miss" he replied and marched towards in the indicated direction. Seeing the reputed police officer enter the ward, Anjali, who was sitting next to the patient, stood up abruptly.

"Hello, Mr Singh" greeted Anjali and Rauf.

"Hello, how are you?" asked Mr Singh adjusting his hat.

"Fine sir" spoke Anjali.

"Ok, so again a hit and run case...." Mr Singh commented, looking at the lady who was in deep slumber. She looked like a fresh rose with her peaches & cream skin, round plump face, snub nose and roseate lips. Her ethereal beauty had held everyone captive, including Mr Singh.

"Who brought her here? Did her family members come to see her?" he asked.

"No, Sir. No one knows who she is. The man who brought her here did not find anything with her. No ID proof or mobile phone, nothing. She was lying on the road, that's it" answered Anjali.

"But why is she still not awake? Is the case that critical?" asked Mr Singh.

"She is out of danger, Sir. She should regain consciousness soon" whispered both the attendants.

"Ok then, inform me whenever she returns to the land of living" Mr Singh told them, as they all headed towards the exit leaving the woman alone in the room where she was sleeping tranquilly. They had hardly walked a few steps away from the door, when suddenly a voice rang out saying, "Don't! Please don't!"

"Who is crying out like this? Is it the lady?" asked Mr Singh.

"Oh, my God! She has woken up" Anjali gasped.

Everyone rushed into the ward. The woman was still wailing aloud. Her voice was like a coo-coo bird; her cry was deep enough to attract everyone to who she was audible. In just a few seconds, her face had become damp with tears.

"Hey... Settle down. It's okay. You are in the hospital. Calm down, dear" Anjali said in a low and refined voice, trying to pacify the distressed lady. She kept stroking the lady's forehead gently in a bid to calm her down. A few minutes passed, after which the lady stopped crying and looked up at Anjali, who was smiling at her encouragingly. Rauf rushed to call the doctor.

Mr Singh gently excused Anjali and approached the woman.

"Hello miss, how are you now?" he asked decorously with a benign smile.

"I am fine, but please... please save him! I think he is in danger. Just go and rescue him from wherever he is." The panic-stricken woman cried out, imploring the inspector to rescue a person.

"Who do you want to be rescued?" asked Mr Singh, grasping the seriousness of the matter.

"Ranil..." she whispered smoothly as if that name meant everything to her. Her face had shrunk in agony; her eyes were still for a minute. It looked like she was lost in some other world.

"Ranil? Who is he, ma'am? Can you please elucidate what happened? Give us every minute detail about everything. How did you get into this accident? Please tell us everything you know or remember. I want you to make a detailed statement about this" said Mr Singh, eager to solve the mystery.

"I know nothing! Leave me alone, please leave me alone!" squawked the woman as she became impatient with Mr Singh's questions.

"Okay, miss. As you wish. Relax yourself. I will come later. Take care" Mr Singh said and left the room. Anjali soon came inside and tried to pacify the perturbed patient. She became avid to know everything that had happened with the lady. 'Where had she come from? Who was Ranil? What had happened to him?' All these questions were swirling in Anjali's mind. Dr. Sinha entered the ward followed by Rauf. He inspected the patient's condition and found everything in order. Walking a few steps away from the bed, he called Anjali and said "I think she should be shifted to the general ward. She no longer needs intensive care."

Accordingly, the woman was shifted to the general ward. Apart from the nurses in charge of the ward,

Anjali too began participating in taking care of the patient.

Since the lady's somnolent black eyes were signalling to the slumber she wanted, Anjali made her lay down comfortably. She covered her with a light blanket and came out of the ward where Mr Singh was waiting for her.

"I want her to wake up soon. I need to know about this Ranil. May be, this man is in danger? It's my duty to save him, but how can I till I know where this man is? Also, she hasn't made any formal statement yet" Mr. Singh pondered, burdening his mind by overthinking.

Anjali held his hand tenderly and said, "Don't worry, I am there to help you."

"Hmm.... I trust my fiancée. Whenever she is calm enough to make a statement, inform me."

Saying this, the cop bid goodbye to Anjali and headed outside.

*

"Hey Anjali, what is the condition of that woman now?" asked Kristal, another nurse.

"She is fine now" said Rauf coming from behind.

"She seems to be from a good family" spoke another nurse.

"That is not the topic to be discussed. What is the need of knowing the family background of a person who is to be cured?" Anjali asked in annoyance.

"Anjali... I didn't mean it that ways...."

"Whatever! I am going to see her now. Bye..." said Anjali, quickening her steps towards the room. On reaching there, she saw the lady in a conscious state. Anjali quickly ran to Dr. Sinha's cabin to call him. Dr Sinha entered the room with Anjali and Rauf and came near to the woman. Both the attendants were standing on the other side of the bed.

"Hello dear" spoke Dr Sinha, "How are you feeling now?"

"I am fine now; actually, much better" answered the woman trying to glance around the ward, but her vision was blocked by the translucent curtains on both sides of the bed. The only thing visible to her was a table with medicines spread over it. At last, she looked at Anjali and smiled feebly.

Dr Sinha checked her blood pressure and heartbeats. He smiled and said "Everything is okay."

The woman smiled back.

The doctor strode towards the exit. He beckoned Anjali who was still standing beside the woman, Anjali followed the order and walked towards him.

"Yes sir?" she asked.

"Listen Anjali, inform Mr Singh about the patient having regained consciousness, okay?"

"Fine sir, I will" replied Anjali and walked back to the woman. She was anxious to hurl the volley of queries at the patient, but instead of asking questions which would make her go wild, Anjali started the conversation with some general questions.

"So, what is your name dear?" she asked softly.

The lady who was lying on the bed, tilted her head towards Anjali and moved her rosy lips to speak - "Ruhani."

Yes... she was owner of an undefiled name which echoed in Anjali's ears.

"Ruhani.... Wow, that's a lovely name. So Ruhani, tell me something about yourself. Where are you from? Tell me something about your family... anything... everything..."

"Huhhh...." sighed Ruhani. She was loath to answer Anjali's question, as it was connected to the memories she did not want to recall. Nevertheless, she decided to answer the nurse because as she did not want to be discourteous to such a gracious lady.

"I am from a conservative Muslim family; except my parents, everyone was very orthodox in my family. I belong to a small village of Karla, and Karla village belongs only to our family. It is an aesthetic place; an amalgamation of sand dunes and rocky path which is a home to deer, rabbits, peacocks. Khejris and Rohiras add more beauty to that place. It is a heavenly place; very calm and placid, but now I live with my husband Ranil."

"Ok, it must have been an arranged marriage, isn't it?" asked Anjali.

"Naa naa... Ours was a love marriage. Actually, to tell you the truth, we haven't tied the knot legally yet. We will be doing that soon, but still, I consider him as my husband. I know that's weird" she stated proudly with a wide smile.

"Oh wow... so there is an ingredient of love in your story. Come on, I want to hear it. Tell me everything from your birth to becoming such a drop-dead gorgeous woman" egged on Anjali who always took interest in love stories.

Ruhani chortled; becoming impatient to confide everything, she started speaking fast like a tiny tot. "I was born on 16 March 1994. I was my parent's first child, but except for them, everyone else's face was crestfallen with dejection with the thought that a huge liability had taken birth in their house in my form."

"I know, Ruhani. To understand the ideology of conservatives, you need to have a heart full of hatred. I want to know more about your family."

"We were all in control of 'Baa'."

"Who is Baa?" Anjali interrupted.

"Huh… Baa, my grandfather, a man with words, a nose and reputation. He is a respected man in our clan and among many such conservatives, because he has always played the role of being the 'protector of traditions and prestige', thus making him an object of veneration. Hahaha, a man with nose he is, as if none of us possess this sense organ!"

"Ok, were your clan members not educated?" asked Anjali.

"Well, no one there ever learned anything from their textbooks. Rote learning was their only weapon to score marks, pass exams and carry on with their family businesses. No one ever realized that their books were trying to edify them. Seriously, how could people just swot up things? I was so impressed when I read about Raja Ram Mohan Roy sir in my history book, he inspired me a lot. I realised that social evils in our society still exist because we just study to score good marks...." continued Ruhani, losing the track of the conversation.

"Ahem ahem...." interrupted Anjali, nudging her in the right direction saying "Well Ruhani, you were telling something about your story."

"Oh yes, I am sorry!" Ruhani realized and continued. "So, everyone there studied just for getting a tag of an 'educated person'. Nothing else. I was not a bright student in kindergarten. When I was a pre-primary student I went through many struggles. I was beaten up by my teachers every day. That automatically gave a chance to my classmates to browbeat me until I cried. It was hurtful, but I never dared to speak up about my agony to my family, out of fear. My childhood wasn't a roller-coaster ride. I was always shackled by the horror of my classmates and family. The gift of compassion was only given by my parents and no one else."

"That's sad."

"Awww.... Don't be sad. My teenage came as a miracle. Yes, it was truly a miracle. From an average student, I suddenly turned into a highbrow person. Well, that's what people started calling me! Life was going on, and so was I. My education had succeeded in changing my mentality; my thinking had gone beyond a conservative mindset."

"So then, was that when you found someone good?" asked Anjali, in the hope of getting a positive answer, and the answer she was interested in.

"Yes indeed. Everything was good. We shifted to Jodhpur, 250 km away from my village. We shifted there for my secondary education. I thanked God for this, because finally I was away from the yolk of strait-laced misogynists and bigoted people. Due to my good grades, I got admission in one of the renowned schools of the city.

I adored everything about this *blue city*, but never visited inside the old city where I could actually see the colour 'blue'. I remember, my father planned a secret visit to Mehrangarh fort, which made me damn happy. On that day I realized why Jodhpur was called a 'blue city'! Goshhh... the view of the blue walls hiding their faces with the veil of green Indian lilac trees looked like a newly wedded bride teasing her groom by hiding her beautiful face. It was so mesmerizing!" Ruhani lowered her gaze and kept smiling to herself for some time, perhaps lost in those fond memories of yore.

After a while, Anjali broke her out of the reverie and asked, "Ruhani, what about your school?"

"Well, my school and tuition centre surpassed every other institution of the city - not in case of money, but in education. Apart from getting education, I also got a new family here. I had never experienced such kind of a life. Visiting a friend's home was so uncommon for me earlier; but now, it started becoming a pleasant reality Standing in a group around our parked scooters for chatting endlessly after tuition classes.... going to a fast-food corner to munch some junk food... everything here was so fresh and electrifying. I was cherishing each & every moment of this new life, and had become completely engrossed in exploring those felicitous minutes of my life, till I heard something appalling."

"What was that?" Anjali asked with curiosity writ large on her face.

"I heard that my family was going to get me engaged!"

"What?! Engaged? But you were still in your high secondary, isn't it?" Anjali exclaimed in horror.

"Yes engaged! That too, to a person who I always considered as my brother. They were doing so to revamp the relation which had deteriorated. The engagement was happening to bring sweetness in the relation with the people whom they once considered as their foe. I was the one who was put at stake; they never once thought of asking for my opinion. I was inconsolable during the entire engagement ceremony. I cried, I shouted, I tried everything to remonstrate against the utterly unfair decision but no one heard my pleas or shrieks! It was as if they had collectively jammed cotton-buds of honour in their ears and they never wanted to throw those out.

The engagement ceremony was held in my village house. My parents lied that we are going there for attending a small family function. The small journey caused me headache. Arghh! It was a really intolerable one. When we reached there, I saw the house filled with merriment; each member of the house was busy doing some work. Fragrance of marigold and roses together was rejuvenating the milieu, while relieving my headache too. Suddenly, I felt a slight push from behind. It was my elder cousin brother Hassan, carrying a heavy mat. On the other side, Parvez bhaiya was instructing the light decorator, shouting at him in a loud voice. One portion of the house was turned into cooking area.

The confectioner was spinning 'moong dal ka halwa' with his slotted spoon in a huge karahi. From its aroma, I got the idea of the halwa being nectareous. Haha my sweet tooth made me stare at the dish for a while.

"Are you going to eat this halwa with your eyes, Ruhani? Let it get cooked first" my favourite cousin Heena chortled as she approached me. My face sparkled looking at her. I embraced her and we both went into a room where no one could distract us from our long conversation. I initiated the topic to be discussed, but she seemed disinterested. Instead, she gave me a mischievous smile and started teasing me by taking the name of Imran, my second cousin. At first her words puzzled me, but then I thought she must be joking. I laughed at her and also praised her efforts to frighten me. Suddenly some girls entered the room and asked me 'what will be my attire for engagement ceremony.' The reality started sinking in my heart. Terrified, I quickly sensed the upcoming threat!

I rushed out from the room and ran to my mother for confirming the validity of what those girls were saying. She was quiet and looked at me helplessly; her reaction didn't surprise me. Just then, one of my paternal aunts commanded me - "Wear a nice pair of shalwar-kameez; your in-laws are on the way."

Shivering in fear I felt like a prey who was ensnared by those predators through deception.

I became fidgety and restless when confronted with the reality. I remember rushing towards the sand dunes to hide myself when the ceremony was about to start. My aunt and elder cousin brother followed me like bloodhounds! They clutched my wrists and hauled me back to the abode of the dead. Those ferocious beasts took me back at warp speed to that tophet. They made me sit on a small wooden platform. I was straining to unclasp my wrists from their mucky hands, but I didn't have that much strength.

I was howling in agony, but none of them was tender enough to feel the affliction I was suffering from. Everyone was involved in relishing the ceremony. That moment was too poignant for me. They covered my head with a red dupatta. One of the aunts of my so-called fiancé forcibly opened my mouth and crammed some jaggery into it. Later, she made me drink a teaspoon of ghee. I spat that stuff on her face out of anger. Her facial expression indicated that she wanted to slap me hard but her need to maintain her image, resisted her from doing so. The women present there were flabbergasted with my act and began whispering among themselves. My mother, who was standing a few steps away, looked at me with contempt. This obviously motivated the woman to behave aggressively. She gave me a grisly look and grabbed my hand to tie a sacred thread around my wrist. I struggled to remove her hand but she made her grip tighter, hurting me devilishly. The onlookers started singing - *"Le jayengai, le jayengai dilwale dulhaniya le jayengai"*. Their hoarse voices were banging on my ears. I wanted to shut them up and slap them so hard that their mouths would get paralyzed, but the only thing I was able to do was groan over my vulnerable condition. After accomplishment of the ceremony, I quietly stood up like a lifeless being. Every village girl of my age was congratulating me. Huh... how could people congratulate me on my death?! I pushed everyone aside and walked straight into a room. Not a single person cared to share my torment or accompany me to mourn over the hardship I went through. I was flung alone with my grief-stricken condition. On that day I realized that those folks were dead inside. These putrid rituals still persist because no one wants to ruin their image. Those people will readily destroy their lives but not their image. Following what their elders taught them - even if those things are exploitive - is their way of showing respect to the elders. Some people don't go against this norm because they consider it as their fate. Weeping over my pain, I fell asleep and forgot everything when I woke up.

In spite of whatever happened, I made myself unswerving, saying 'everything will be okay, don't get influenced by these people.' I remember, once my cousin had told me that the person with whom I was engaged doesn't consider me as his cousin sister anymore and wants to marry me. Those words had startled me. How could a boy change so much in just a few days, I wondered!

"Then? What happened?" asked Anjali. "Did you convince yourself that it was your fate?"

"No, never! Not at all!" shouted Ruhani, "I would have rather died!"

"Oh, you never felt like talking to your fiancée!?"

"What are you saying? Who fiancée? I never saw him like that. I remember, when I created my account on Facebook, he had sent me friend request, but I blocked him immediately."

"Oh, you were engaged so early! What about marriage?" asked Anjali totally confounded by the patient's talk.

"Huh... marriage! In our society, early engagement is a way to reserve a child. That forceful engagement turns into marriage after the child attains legal age. Parents don't allow their child to talk to the person with whom they are engaged. Each of my cousin sisters went with flow and got married to the person who was reserved for them. My case was like chalk & cheese; I never accepted their dominance over my life. My life is 'my life'? Can anyone else die in my place and gift me his breath? No... no one can do that! Then why should I give right to someone else over my breath? The problem with people's mentality is that we want to control our children instead of guiding them."

"Hmm... that's true. What happened after that?" asked Anjali

"Nothing, I came back to Jodhpur with my parents. I was very angry with them. I didn't speak a word to them for the next few days. I wanted to horrify them and make them feel guilty hence I didn't touch even a morsel of food for three days."

"Oh dear, food was not your culprit" said Anjali with care in her voice.

"Actually, I was eating everything secretly. Shirley would come to visit me with delicious food packed in aluminium foils. It was her idea to pretend as if I am not eating anything. My parents, however, did feel bad. Many a times, they tried to explain the whole situation and convinced me to continue to live my life as I was living earlier, forgetting the day of engagement. Many a times I pleaded my father saying, "Paa, if I score good grades in my exams, will you break my engagement?" But of the matter of retaining his reputation overshadowed his fatherhood, "Let's not talk about this" was the only answer he had.

I had no option but to accept my fate. In school I started considering myself as a different person from all my fellow friends. They weren't chained as I was. Thinking about them I had only one thought swirling in my head - "How lucky they are." They are free, their young minds can think about something innovative rather than taking the load of a forced relation. I was ill-fated; the one traumatized between the two worlds wherein the first world shockingly asked - "What? You are engaged!" and the other chided - "What? You are not engaged yet!" I myself was part of first world, rational and liberal.

Chapter 2
Learning to live, again

"My engagement became my biggest secret, but there was no sense in thinking about it anymore. I had my studies to think about. After a few days of mental suffering, I gulped my pain and continued with my regular schedule of school, coaching classes, homework, and tests. I surrounded my life with the things which were crucial for me at that point of time.... and then... then, came a moment which thrilled me!"

"And what was that?" Anjali asked curiously, slowly pulling the blanket over Ruhani's feet.

"The advent of Ranil in my life..." sighed Ruhani's, her eyes filled with tears no less than pearls - precious, very precious.

Anjali held her hand and wiped her face saying, "Tell me everything Ruhani; it will lessen your pain."

At long last, Ruhani started speaking. "It was last day of the year. I was busy struggling with the questions thrown at me in the coaching institute.

My institute didn't have high-class decoration. It had small classrooms, and cream-coloured benches. The front wall had a blackboard which always gave us and our tutor an asthma attack. The entry and exit doors were at our back. That day, suddenly the door of banged loudly making a head-splitting noise. Everyone looked back to see the person responsible for that deafening sound. As soon as I turned around, I noticed the person already staring at me. For a moment, our eyes got locked on each other. Then I quickly escaped from that awkward eye contact by again turning to face the writing board. He was Ranil, a handsome boy with a smiling face, dusky skin, toned physique. He was coming inside in his own rhythm ignoring our reaction on his act. Ranil was our senior and one of those students who was too much friendly with our tutor. He had a short conversation with our tutor and went back to his classroom. An hour passed. My class was over. I stood up and started walking towards the exit till I was stopped by a voice from the back, "Are you coming to New Year's party tomorrow? It's going to held here, in this institute" he asked. I looked back to see who it was. It was Ranil; he was smiling mischievously at me, "Oh God! This boy is such a barefaced" I thought, ignored him, and left the place.

"Wow, you should have replied to him. It was rude on your part."

"Actually, he was teasing. A genuine invitation sounds different. I had a habit of throwing audacious remarks, but he was lucky to get my silence as a reply. But on the very next day, Ranil again passed a moronic comment on me at the coaching institute, and from that day probably, I started abhorring him. I also told my tutor that the boy is an eve teaser, but instead of supporting me, the tutor defended him saying that the boy was struggling with his health from last few months. He had recently undergone an operation for liver transplantation. It was because of the operation that he had joined the institute so late. Yet, his performance was better in comparison with those students who joined during initial days. My tendency of being an empathetic person reached its peak in his case. It made me feel apologetic for whatever I spoke about him, even though I knew he was wrong.

At the successive day at school, like every other day I was surrounded by my friends outside the classroom during recess. We were shouting, delivering asinine statements and laughing at our own waggish behaviour. The edifice of my school was alluring; there was an empty space in between the corridors for a lush lawn. Eventually my eyes rolled to the upper corridor and suddenly halted on a familiar face. I saw him again. "Oh, my God, this boy is in my school!! Such a dullard." I was stunned. I was staring at him and at the same moment, he also looked at me. I escaped from that situation by rushing inside the classroom.

Next day, being monitor of my class I was managing my class in the assembly hall, shouting 'maintain proper one hand distance' and 'slightly to the left or right'. It was my daily morning job. Suddenly Shirley, my best friend approached me and complained about the senior boys who had joined our class's line. Feeling like a protector, I headed towards those boys and called at top of my voice "Are you all dopey to not notice that you all have joined 10th class's line?" One of them turned around; you can guess who he was! As soon as I saw him, I started walking in the reverse direction without uttering a single word. The next moment I wondered why I was unable to speak anything in front of him? Why did a girl like me behave in such a dumb manner? It was strange! I had never behaved like this earlier.

On the way from the assembly hall to our class, Shirley came running towards me, breaking the line.

"Hey...Ruhani..." she called.

"Shirley ...join the line...please...go!" I scolded.

"I will...but tell me, who was that senior boy? Hmm...?" she said teasing me.

"Oh.... Who...? I don't know him. Why are you asking me about him?"

"Don't hide anything, Ruhani. I can sense your feelings before your confession."

"Shut up Shirley." I spoke harshly because that time I really hated Ranil (according to my mind).

Shirley smirked at me and entered the class. After listening to the endless lectures, eventually the final bell rang putting a full stop on the prosy chapters which we were tackling. Shirley and I headed towards our school bus, kept our bag inside and came out to tittle-tattle with our undisputed gossip queens. We were standing in a group when abruptly, Shirley started shouting my name loudly - "Ruhani... Ruhani..."

I was puzzled, because I was standing right beside her. "Why is she shouting like that?" I wondered. Soon, my confusion was unclogged when I saw Ranil standing a few steps away from us with his friends. I don't know why, but when I looked at him, I felt butterflies fluttering in my stomach, my heart started pounding fast. He was looking at me. I thought he might have told them foul things about me to besmirch my character because his friends were continuously ogling at me. After observing me, they looked at Ranil and patted him on the back. I was watching them keenly but pretending like 'I don't know if they are noticing me or someone else?' It was difficult to hear Ranil but I noticed his lip sync. He said - "ru..ha..ni.". Confusion struck my mind again. Why did he take my name? Well, he must have pointed at me to tell his friends that he teased me at the coaching institute. "He might be a quick-witted person, but lacks probity" I thought.

'pohhh..pohhh...' The school bus blew the horn giving a signal for departure. I and Shirley quickly stepped inside the bus and sat on our seats.

"Ruhani..." spoke Shirley.

"Hmm....?"

"You know what, that boy was noticing you, and, now he also knows your name. Congrats, thank me later for this. He is so good looking. I can imagine your kids now itself! Wow!"

"Stop it Shirley, he is no less than a wind-up merchant. He was poking fun at me with his friends" I spoke angrily.

"How do you know that? Maybe he was telling them that he likes you."

"What?!"

"Yes...you know, boys tease only those girls who they like. Today morning I was standing near him, but he didn't say anything to tease me. In fact, he didn't look at me even once. He is not at all depraved. He was simply standing behind me. I complained to you because it was our class's line, that's it" said Shirley defending him.

"Huh... Shirley, you always end up being a kvetcher. Well leave, but how do you know the 'teasing fact'? I asked.

"I Googled it...! '15 signs to know if the boy likes you.' Hahahaha!"

"Oh really!!" I asked with a poker face. "Shut up Shirley, why do even you search such kind of irrelevant stuff?"

"Ruhani... it's because I want to confirm whether my crush likes me or not. So..."

"Oh, my God....! Shirley, he doesn't even look at you."

"Ruhani...how can you say that? You are a pessimist! Look at me, how optimistic I am about you and that senior boy."

"I am not a pessimist. I got to know that your crush is already in a relationship with a girl from another school."

"Ruhani, that is not true."

"Shirley, believe me, I haven't told you about this because I thought your feelings are temporary."

"What? Are you serious? Is it true?" Shirley was shocked. Her facial expressions showed the heartbreak she felt.

"Shirley...it's ok, he was just a crush."

"Hmm.... I am habituated to going through such crush breakups. Hope that girl behaves like a witch!"

"Witch? But why?"

"Ruhani, her bad behaviour will give me peace that the boy is dating someone who can't match my level and I was the perfect match for him, but he doesn't deserve me" explained Shirley pouring out her grudge.

"Shirley... be cool... it happens."

"I don't mind, I will get better" she said and started laughing.

Just then, the bus applied brakes abruptly and we experienced Newton's First Law of Motion. I stepped out of the bus, waved at Shirley and entered my house. After having my lunch and a short nap, I walked to my institute, but today my mind was feeling distracted; my eyes were starving for one glimpse of Ranil. I don't know why? I was looking at the door again and again. But unfortunately, he was missing from the scene. I felt sad. I knew I hated him but then why was I waiting just to have one glance of his?

At night, as I went off to my bed and closed my eyes, I saw Ranil smiling at me. Abruptly I opened my eyes wide. "Stop it, stupid mind.... let me sleep. Stop thinking about him, I hate him." I scolded my mind, but it proved to be a futile act, cause my brain and heart had already planned a conspiracy against me; a conspiracy to think about Ranil constantly. For sake of diverting my mind from Ranil, I opened a music player app on my phone and played my favourite song-

"Pehla pehla pyaar hai,

pehli pehli baar hai,

jaan ke bhi anjaana,

aisa mera yaar hai!"

I felt shy listening to the lyrics of the song. I was feeling as if the lyricist had written each and every line thinking of me only. "Is this love...?" I asked myself.

It was 3 AM and I was still awake. Finally, after an hour, the windows of my eyes were shut, but in spite of that I managed to wake up at 6 A.M. I showered, wore my uniform, combed my hair, but this time I pulled out some hair flicks to enhance my look. My mother noticed my new look. she even gave me a favourable remark but her compliment was not convincing me because her facial expression was contradictory to what she said. She gave me boiled eggs for breakfast. I ate them hastily, proceeded out of the house and waited for my school bus.

'pohh... pohhh.' The bus arrived and I sat beside Shirley. On reaching the school, everyone walked to their classes. Shirley and I stepped inside our classroom where only one student was present. We called him 'Sanatta' (silence) as he never talked to anyone.

"We came so early today!" I exclaimed.

"Hmm.... okay, I am going to washroom, are you coming with me?" Shirley asked.

"Shirley, we have stepped in the school just few minutes ago."

"Ruhani...I want to see my face in the mirror, because you are looking striking today! Yes, I have noticed those hair flicks on your face; what's the matter? You never come like this to school? Haa...?" Shirley teased me.

"Shirley, you have a one-tracked thinking. Can't I do it for myself?"

"Yes...you can... Well, okay then... I am going to the washroom." Shirley said and left the place.

"Huh..." I sighed and sat on the chair smiling and thinking of Ranil. Sanatta was looking at me in a freakish way. I realized my unusual behaviour and controlled my expressions.

"Ruhani......come fast...." Shirley came running to me. Clasping my hand, she pulled me to make me stand and asked to follow her.

"What happened Shirley? Where are we going?" I asked. Her behaviour annoyed me; it diverted my mind from thinking about Ranil to thinking about the reason she was pulling me for.

"Hasshh... that's it." she said pausing in the corridor.

"What?" I asked running my eyes over the corridor to see what she wanted to show me.

"Look up." She said pointing to the upper corridor.

"Ssshh....don't do it." I said, flicking her hand which was pointing at Ranil. When I looked at him, I was half exultant and half jittery.

"Ouch...Ruhani, you hurt me!"

"Shirley ...why don't you understand? It's not good to point your finger at someone like that. What will he think?"

"Ruhani..." Shirley whispered.

"Hmm... what?"

"He is looking at you" Shirley spoke slowly, as if a ghost was looking at me.

My heart was in my throat. Taking a deep breath, I turned my face towards Ranil. He was looking at me without blinking his eyes, and waved his hand to say 'hi'. I greeted him back and quickly looked back at Shirley with a blush on my cheeks. Shirley was giving me a mischievous look, which brought a coy smile to my face. My heart became like a cat on a hot tin roof because it was experiencing its beat becoming unstable.

"Haww...Ruhani are you blushing? Gosh.... you are in love!"

"Please Shirley, I am not!"   I replied trying to avoid the topic.

"No, don't deny it. You so are" Shirley said confidently.

"Think whatever you want to. I don't care. How many times I have to tell you that this is pure poppycock and I will never share my focus with such kind of claptrap. If you are finding him dishy then go, grab him. The doors are open; no one will thwart your actions." I lashed out at Shirley to vindicate her claim. I know I was wrong for being so harsh on her, but she didn't say a single angry word. Instead she laughed and spoke. " No, I don't want to be his paramour, I can't stab my best friend." Winking at me, she smirked. Such an unrepentant girl she was. I hope she still possesses the same nature. I miss her a lot." Travelling back to her schooldays and reminiscing about the past made Ruhani's eyes sparkle with tears.

Walking out from the past she continued. "On the same day our school was having a ceremony of announcing the names of the head girl, head boy and other council members. All the students were summoned and assembled in the assembly hall. We were standing in a queue maintaining pin drop silence. Our principal walked to the stage, stood near the podium and started with her same old dialogue " How are you students? I hope you all must be fine." later she started announcing the names of the council members. Shirley and I were standing at the back; apathetic to watching the ceremony. We didn't allow ourselves to get blended with the pupils who were drooling over the mind-numbing programme. Shirley began yawning. She looked at me helplessly with red sleepy eyes and made a hilarious face at our principal. I chuckled looking at her face and encouraged her to tolerate the Principal's words for few more minutes.

"Ruhani, I don't know why she always starts her speech like that. She questions us about us, and gives the answers herself" Shirley giggled.

"Hehe... Stop it Shirley. Princy will definitely kill you if she finds you talking."

"Huh, my tricks for speaking can never betray me. Just keep your one finger over your nose, other fingers over your mouth, and start gazing at her like she is your lover. Now act like you are listening to her attentively."

"Hahaha...let's not show this much contempt for her. Focus on the ceremony now."

"Blue house captain.... Ranil Daga." announced the principal, making a jolt run through my being.

"OMG! OMG...! Ruhani, look there, your Romeo is on the stage" Shirley exulted pointing at Ranil again.

"Oh… that senior boy….so his name is Ranil. Hmmm, nice name, hehehe." I laughed. "Wow Shirley, he is the blue house captain."

"Congrats Ruhani, your Romeo is an all-rounder. Gosh... look at his hair. In the morning he was looking good, but now his hair is looking like he suffered a 440-volt current! Have you touched him Ruhani? Hahaha!"

"Shut up Shirley. He styled his hair. This style is called spikes."

"Oho... why are you defending him?"

"I am not!" I argued in my defence.

The 40 minutes of the formal procedure was over, and with it our chat too.

On the same day I went to Shirley's home. she wanted to show me something. We were sitting in her room and were gazing at the computer screen. She logged in to her Facebook account.

"Wooo Shirley! You have an account on Facebook!!"

"Yes, of course, everyone can't be fogey like you. Now don't disturb me. So what was his name again? Ranil Daga.... ? Let's search him now" spoke Shirley and typed Ranil's name on search column. The results showed him on the top. "Hmm... Wow, look at his display picture!" she exclaimed and looked at me. "Hawww... Ruhani you are ogling at his picture!"

"Huh... no.. no... I was checking out the message on his T-shirt."

"That blurred message?" Shirley asked poker-faced. "I understand everything dear. Nothing to hide now. Let us check his relationship status" she added and clicked on 'About' option. "OMG.... congrats Ruhani, he is single. Yeahhh...!"

"What? He is single!?" Shirley and I started grooving without music, and of course without thinking that most the singles on social sites are secretly mingled.

"Yes, that means there is no obstacle between you and him. The track is clear. Go for it, Ruhani."

'*Kaise mai kahoon tujhse, rehna hai tere dil mein.*' Shirley started singing loudly. Well, 'singing' would be a wrong word for what she was doing. It was more of screeching! I quickly kept my hand over her mouth to stop her from singing (read – screeching) stridently.

"Shut up, Shirley! What do you mean by 'go for it'? I don't want to get myself indulged in all these thankless tasks; my academic performance is my top priority."

"Stop it Ruhani, who is telling you to make him your boyfriend? Least you can do is make him a friend; perhaps, best friend. Hey, but don't make him reach to my level."

"Haha.. Shirley, no one can replace you!"

"Should I send him friend request?" Shirley asked, opening her eyes wide.

"Will he accept? He doesn't know you."

"Don't worry about that. Have a look at my profile picture, it includes you too. Look, you and me are posing together; he will definitely accept my friend request" she said, winking at me.

"Good idea, Shirley. Am I looking good in this picture?"

"Of course. Now be quiet. You are frittering away my time; let me send him request first." She pressed on the 'Add Friend' option and started bouncing in excitement. "Oh my God... I sent him friend request, oh my God."

"Calm down Shirley, you have just sent him friend request. He hasn't accepted it yet."

"Ruhani....wait, there is a notification, let me check." She became serious and clicked on the icon.

"What happened?" I asked. My heart was in my mouth when she clicked on the notification icon.

"He has accepted!! Yippiee...." She yelled and started bouncing again.

"What?" I was amazed. That moment was so rollicking, it made me bounce with her. We checked his each and every status and photo thoroughly. "Who is this girl Shirley?" I asked looking at his photo wherein he had posed with a girl.

"Arghhh... Ruhani... you are sounding like an envious vamp. Chill... she must be his friend."

"Fine, I am not all envious of her."

During those days my school hours were in full swing. I became meticulous about my appearance. Shirley started noticing the metamorphosis I was going through. My hairstyle was altered from oily tight plates to shampooed high pony tail; the singular talcum powder lying on my dressing table was now accompanied by kohl, coloured lip balms and perfumes. I became fond of going to school with a hope of getting one glance of Ranil. After all, the embellishment of my looks was only for him. My mission proved unbeaten whenever he looked at me. Those days made me realize the importance of the lines *"Jab tak na pade aashiq ki nazar, shringhaar adhura rehta hai"*. His look was so intense that it made me feel like I am the most beautiful girl he had ever seen. His absence made my heart spiritless. I wanted to have at least one glimpse of his every day and wanted him to look back, because he was the only boy I wanted to gaze at me.

After a few days I went to my friend's house who I had met during an inter-school dance competition. I shouted her name from outside her house "Meera". Listening to my call someone came out and headed towards me with a smiling face. At that moment my heart felt like it is the wispiest object on this earth, and my face lit up with a smile. That person was playing role of iron for my heart of magnet. The person was Ranil! "What is he doing here?" I wondered as he came near me and we had an introductory conversation. Later, Meera came out and introduced me to her cousin. After that incident, a chain of meetings just sparked off unexpectedly.

Days passed but we never talked to each other like friends normally do. It was perhaps because we both had a shy nature. Even a simple 'Hi' from him would make me happy.

Every morning after reaching school, I would become eager to go to the assembly hall, but Shirley was fed up of the pesky duty she was performing for me during the assembly time.

"Shirley, is he looking at me?" I whispered standing behind Shirley in the queue.

"Wait... let me check." She replied and looked behind to see Ranil. "No, his eyes are closed."

"Oh... now? Did he open his eyes?"

"I don't know."

"Then look at him and tell me."

"I won't! Now be quiet and focus on chanting the prayer. These all are illusions of the world.... *Itni shakti hume dena daata, mann ka vishawas kamzor ho naa.*" Shirley commented and began saying the prayer in a loud voice.

"Listen Shirley, are you not my best friend? Please check if he is looking at me or not... for the last time, please."

"Okay, for the last time." She spoke, opened her eyes and looked behind to check out Ranil. But as soon as she turned around, she saw our class teacher standing in front of her.

"What's the matter? I am observing you for the last few minutes. I was not aware of the fact that assembly hall is a place to check out the senior boys! Also, if you can't sound mellifluous while singing the prayer then keep your mouth mum. No need to create a mess by screeching here. Look at Ruhani, she didn't open her eyes even once. All her focus is on chanting the name of God. Huh." Our class teacher chastised Shirley for being glaikit. Shirley didn't utter a single word to her and quietly gulped all those humiliating words just for me.

When our class teacher left, I looked behind and gave her a rueful grin. She started chuckling and closed her eyes. But my madness didn't stop there. I always waited for the recess bell to ring so that I could stand outside the classroom and look fixedly at Ranil. In every period, I asked for permission to go to the washroom just to roam in the corridor where his class was situated. Walking by his classroom it became our habit to quickly peep inside the room. Many a times, I would get lucky to see Ranil, even though for a second.

During those days, Shirley and I started coming late to the school on her two-wheeler. It was intentional, because many a times we found Ranil standing in the late-comers' queue. It became my duty to accompany him. Even though he was a house captain but punishment was same for all. I knew 'his bike', so Shirley started parking her scooter beside Ranil's bike whenever she found an empty space there. When the final bell rang, we waited near the parking lot for Ranil to come and notice us, but every time that boy simply waved his hand to say 'bye' and nothing else. In spite of that I was happy; at least my eyes were getting relief by seeing him. God, how crazy I was for him!

Thus, many days passed in the same manner. The relation between me and Ranil was still limited to a 'crush', but one day, things changed all of a sudden.

I got a call from an unknown number.

"Hello."

"Hello, is this Ruhani?"

"Yes, who's this?"

"Ranil." he answered.

Hearing the name, I experienced combined feelings of exultation and stupefaction. I was unable to speak anything, my mind went blank. I explored my mind's dictionary but found it hard to search an apropos word to speak which could have befitted the situation.

"Hello...Ruhani... Are you there?" he asked.

"Yes... yes... Ranil." I replied staggering.

"Actually, Shirley gave me your number, she said that you are facing some problems in mathematics and you wanted me to teach you for some days. What happened? Is our coaching tutor not explaining the subject properly?"

"Aahhhh..." I cursed Shirley for telling him this lie. "Actually, Ranil he explains well ... but you know, he doesn't have extra time to clear the concepts again" I spoke hastily shaking my leg out of nervousness.

"Okay... no issues, we will sit in the coaching centre for an extra hour. I will explain you everything, don't worry" he said and disconnected the call.

My heart beat was audible to me, my lips were dried up, and my breath had stopped for a moment. Normalizing myself I thought - "He disconnected the call so early? Doesn't he hold any feelings for me? I don't think he is interested in me; he just wants his junior to clear her concepts in mathematics. Oh, my God, I don't think he likes me." That time I felt need of calling my 'partner in over thinking'. I called up Shirley and scolded her for an hour but she was brazened enough to not apologise a bit. Instead, she laughed at my situation as she always did. But from within, I was blessing Shirley for whatever she did. She convinced me that somewhere Ranil too holds special feelings for me. Her words were motivating me to walk on the track which was taboo for me.

In the evening I went to my coaching centre. After attending the class, I headed towards the exit.

"Hey… Ruhani!" shouted Ranil.

I stopped and turned around.

"You forgot! Come let's sit there. Take out your mathematics book" he said.

Butterflies were loaded in my breadbasket. Tightening my fist, I looked at his face trying best to not to give him any hint about my inner condition. Quietly, I just followed his instructions. He started clearing my concepts, but who the hell was focusing on his teaching! I was noticing the way he talked, the way he was looking at me. Finishing his lecture, he looked at me and asked "I hope your concepts are clear now." Listening to his words I quickly came out from my thoughts and nodded my head to answer him in the positive.

"Ok, we will continue tomorrow. Bye!" he said and started walking towards the exit. I stood up and packed my bag, still astounded and trying to make myself believe that the incident held veracity. Ranil was actually sitting beside me. When I reached home, I quickly rang Shirley to tell her each and every thing I had felt during that lovely session.

"Don't worry Ruhani, he cleared your concepts. That means he actually cares about you" Shirley assured me.

"Really, but Shirley, even I would have done this for my junior."

"Ruhani, you are an eccentric person! It is crystal clear that he is interested in you and you are taking it as his friendly gesture. Don't do this; use your unused mind."

"Oh... Okay, but what next?"

"Nothing, let things happen the way they are happening. Be normal. Don't try to ruin everything by over thinking; it will work as adding fuel in the fire. And, one more thing; never give him any hint about your fondness for him. Be sure about his feelings first, let him make the first move."

"Ok, I understood everything - behave normally, not give him any hint, and wait for him to initiate. But Shirley, are we not over thinking?"

"Shut up Ruhani. Keep quiet now. You don't know anything about this; I am an experienced person."

"Yes, that's why you are still single. Hahaha!"

"Do you want me to help you, or should I disconnect the call?"

"Sorry Shirley, can't you tolerate a mere joke of mine?"

"Ok... ok... now listen."

Shirley and I continued to talk for more than an hour. From that day, my feelings for Ranil began to escalate and coated my heart like a creeper which covers a house from all sides.

Though Ranil and I were spending some time in the coaching institute for extra studies, but apart from that too, we were doing many other things. We talked on many crucial issues and discussed them with great concern. I enjoyed bantering with him, my comfort level with him was amazing. The velocity of each moment spent with him matched with the velocity of an aerolite. Time drifted forward minimizing the difference between both of us.

Soon after, we started texting each other. Talking to him was such a magical experience for me. Exactly at 9:00 P.M I used to walk upstairs, as it was the time to receive a call from my special one. I felt fortune running towards me when the night sky, in tandem with stars, embellished itself with full moon. Showering under the bracing moonlight I used to wait for his call. It became my habit to brainstorm about sentences I would speak to him; however, after receiving his call all my anticipated planned conversation would only remain a part of my imagination. I don't know why I had smile on my face every second when we talked.

But then with passing time, I saw his topics drifting towards erotic fantasies, which I found perturbing. In spite of that, I got involved in those talks, as I feared that he would leave me if I don't. I wanted him to ask me about my dreams, my likes and dislikes, and future plans. I wanted to have meaningful and deep conversations with Ranil, but it didn't seem to be happening anytime soon.

Filled with fear to express my current feelings, once when I finally confronted Ranil saying that only thing we talk about is sex, he reacted just as I had anticipated. Hitting the roof, he said 'Don't play games with me. You are same as other girls, who only knows to play blame games.' Aghast listening to his words my heart was squeezed; feeling enormous pain, it cried in silence. Playing games? And me! He took me totally wrong. I was just being real. I wanted to express my opinion. I tried explaining to him that I used the word 'We' and not 'He', but Ranil's anger restricted him from understanding my intention. He added that 'if I had come into his life just to trap him in the feeling of being guilty, then the doors of exit from his life were always open'. You know, he did not just add those words but also the agony. Sensing that one more word from my mouth and I would be out from his life I tried to cool his temper. I simply said sorry. The water was muddy now; trying to explain myself further would have just triggered him more.

But I think my acceptance just served to heighten his expectations. After few days, he asked for my nudes, which I denied and received same reaction. He was agitated and blew me with messages that 'I don't trust him and it proves that there is nothing special between two of us. I hurt him...' and so on. In spite of receiving lamentable messages, this time I told him that I am a shy person and never opened up myself like this even in front of my own mother. Ranil found it hard to tolerate my response. Consequently he didn't talk to me for next two days. I apologised to him more than a hundred times in those two days. I explained to him that I had never been in a relationship earlier, and hence never thought that these things were an inescapable part of it. For me, a relationship only meant being emotionally available for someone, motivating them, and making them feel blissful.

"And your relationship wasn't going according to what you thought. Right?" Anjali spoke quickly, smirking at Ruhani.

"Maybe you are right. But no, it wasn't about the relationship. Actually, I think I had my own version of his personality, expecting him to be the same as me, but it wasn't true. I always faced this fact when I talked about my expectations and my opinion. Most of the times my words were totally perceived in contrast to my intentions."

"Ruhani, haven't you ever felt that you should reveal the faults in his personality?"

"No, never, because I knew it would upset him and he might decide to leave me. I was afraid to lose him. It was impossible for me to imagine my life without him. His advent brought so much positivity in me. Why would I think of creating a mess? Even my engagement had become a forgotten event of my life."

"Hmmm... so you never found Ranil's behaviour manipulative towards you?"

"Well, sometimes I did, but if I thought, if I don't stand with my partner, who else will? I mean, yes he did have anger issues, but what is the meaning of love if you only love your partner's good side but not the shady one?"

"Oh, I agree with you. Obviously, it should be unconditional love, but a shady side cannot be covered up with a sparkly cloth just because it belongs to one's partner. It's good to show his dim side without living in terror of being abandoned. If you are on thin ice about his stability in your life then it's time to think, does he really care for you or love you?"

Hearing Anjali's words, Ruhani lay still on her bed. She felt perplexed with the words of the wise lady; she was realising her mistake in having been so docile.

"Hey! Don't think so much! It was just my opinion. He is your husband now, so relax!" said Anjali, adding, "Actually, I have a habit of observing while talking, so sorry for that. I know you must have not got a chance of speaking about Ranil's shady side. Don't feel any kind of guilt for not sharing that with me. I mean, it's totally okay sometimes to pour out your pain, even if it's from your loved ones. Not in front of everyone though. You don't have to worry; I won't fill your ears with words of rage against your husband. Not leaving, but growing and understanding is the solution to all the problems between couples, and for that you need to be expressive. Of course, the other person also needs to respond; not react."

"True, I never shared such thoughts with anyone, not even with Shirley or Ozil, as I don't want anyone to judge my partner and doubt my choice. He was awesome, I know that!"

"Hmm... I adore you for being like that, standing staunchly by your partner. Well, I am relishing the memories of your school days with Ranil, so tell me more about your connection. Would you ever meet each other beyond school or coaching institute?"

"Yeah, we did, on one foggy day of January. Ranil and I decided to go to Jaswant Thada, a magnificent cenotaph, made of elaborately carved marble sheets. It is a phenomenal example of human creation. Sitting beside the lake with our face towards the golden glow of the sun we both felt warmth presented to us by nature. What was more mesmerizing? When Ranil held my hand, protecting me from that chilly morning. All these beautiful things together gave me a soothing aura, creating a soporific effect. I can still feel his words spoken that day, echoing in my mind..."

"Ruhani..." Plucking a leaf from a rose plant planted beside him, he whispered.

"Hmm..."

"It's not the first time that I have been in a relationship. I had two relations before this, one for 6 months, and other for 1 year. Whores they were, both of them. They cheated on me. I was not hurt by my first girlfriend, but the second one, her act actually killed me.

"You had two relationships already at this age?" I asked in shock.

"Hehe, why? Haven't you had any? What is so shocking in that?"

"No, you are my first. I mean I am still a kid. Hehe."

"How old are you? 16? Girls of your age are getting pregnant these days."

"Hehe, yeahh..." I faked my laugh as I didn't like what he said. Then I asked him, "So, Ranil, why did they cheat on you?"

"God knows, some people do get bored of the same face perhaps..." he mused.

"Well, what does love have to do with face?" I asked squinting my eyes.

Looking at me with a strange expression, he smiled and said, "Not everyone asks that question." Then, he held my hand and said, "I have never met anyone like you. So different you are. Unique, beautiful, intelligent and trustworthy .... everything that I wanted in my partner."

His words made my eyes shine. I was happy to know that I stood out from his past girlfriends, who were whores, and I... I was special for him, different from everyone!

Unable to tolerate a particular word 'whore', Anjali quickly exclaimed "Oh! Cheating is such a sin but what actually made them cheat? Sorry to say but everyone has their own version of the story. It is so easy to throw the blame at others and play the victim card. Whore is a strong word to be used for someone."

"Yeah... I mean yes, I don't know their side of the story, just Ranil's...." Ruhani spoke feeling underconfident, probably guilty of agreeing with the word used for another woman who she had never met.

Anjali grasped Ruhani's vibes. To bring her out of her dull mood she brushed the topic aside and said, "Ranil must be feeling lucky to have a girl like you, isn't it?"

"Obviously, I was his 'the one', but that day I felt heavy. It felt as if lots of burden was flung on my shoulder. Gazing at the lake, Ranil abruptly looked at me and spoke "Do you know, Ruhani? Fire and water can never mingle together."

His intention behind this statement bemused my mind. "Ranil? Are you on a scientific track or philosophical?" I asked sensing his intentions, which didn't seem to be a healthy sign for our relation.

"Ruhani....you won't understand." He replied with a bleak expression on his face. His eyes wanted to reveal something, but I don't know what was resisting him to speak his heart out.

"Ranil... I can, and you know what? Fire and water can be together if there is oil between them. If we take the instance of people with different backgrounds, we can see that they can be together if they have trust, respect and immense love." I replied, indirectly mentioning him and me in the situation.

"Hmmm, and I think success plays a vital role if two people from different cultures really want to be together. The people of this society will not be able to resist a person who went against their un-heretical norms. Well, on the other side it's good to squash the feelings before they become intractable. This kind of relation lacks surety. Choosing separate tracks on right time is better than a man becoming an alcoholic and his woman crying a river every night." Saying this Ranil gave me an intense look.

"Ranil, you are still a teenager. Don't go so deep. Your wisdom tooth seems to have started showing its outcome too early! But it is getting difficult to find loyalty in every age group nowadays. You are born under lucky star if you get someone's loyalty. All the obligations of this society are only excuses that we make to feel better if the relationship doesn't last forever. But yes, success is mandatory, I agree." I spoke and looked into his eyes; they were so deep that I almost drowned in them for a minute. I was trying hard to give Ranil a positive outlook as I desperately wanted to be with him, but he was staunch with his ideas and beliefs.

On that day I understood one thing clearly; he was very mature for his age, and that was admirable. I was surely a daydreamer to imagine myself with him in spite of being aware of my conservative background.

There are many saccharine memories of me and Ranil. The first heart-wrenching memory we had was of the farewell given to Grade 12th. On the same day class 10th students were taking their

Practical exams. I was feeling very uneasy that day. Entering through small door of the chemistry lab I accidentally pushed Singhvi Ma'am, our chemistry teacher. Staring at me with her big black eyes, she handed me a piece of paper which had topic of the experiment to be done. Hastily Shirley came in front of me with wide eyes and chapped lips. I sensed her perturbation, and asked-

"What happened Shirley?"

"Ruhani I thoroughly read about all 6 experiments, but the one I skipped is my experiment to be done today."

My mind was already not focused and Shirley had brought a new problem to be solved. Without talking much, I ordered her to initiate the experiment. Then, in a hushed tone, I instructed her about the whole procedure while performing my experiment in tandem. My topic for the exam was observing the action of zinc, iron, copper and aluminium metals for following salt solutions - zinc sulphate, copper sulphate, ferrous sulphate and aluminium sulphate. I wanted to accomplish my task at the soonest. Speedily my hands started working, writing about aims, objectives and concluding the results. I walked straight to Singhvi Ma'am who took my viva, which I totally ruined. At that moment, reaching to Ranil was more important to me. "Ok, leave" ordered Ma'am. I walked out of the lab slowly, and as soon as I reached outside, I ran downstairs like a cheetah I and stopped in front of the gate from where 11th and 12th class students were heading in. I was so eager to have one glance of Ranil, as we had not seen each other since the day we visited Jaswant Thada.

I can't forget that day when for the first time I literally ogled at Ranil! He was looking dapper in a black Jodhpuri suit. Winking, he waved at me from distance. Crossing my arms and taking the support of wall beside me, I smirked. Asking his friends to walk ahead, Ranil walked towards me. I saw his best friend giving him a thumbs up sign.

"Hi, how am I looking?"

Observing him from head to toe I exhaled and said, "Exactly like a prince." My words made his cheeks go red! It was the first time he was receiving such an unabashed compliment from me. He tilted his head adoringly and raised his eyebrows at me with a smile.

"Well... I never saw you looking at me in this way till date" he said. Then, holding my wrist he looked around and suddenly kissed me, or I could say touched my lips for less than a second. Whatever he did, it amazed me. I went quiet and still - unable to react, unable to speak. Finally, the puzzle of *"Chhupana bhi nahi aata, jatana bhi nahi aata"* was solved. It was a gift from him to me as he was treating me the way I wanted to be. He wasn't hiding our relationship from his close ones; it gave me surety from his side. I can't express how much relief I felt that day. I saw him smiling magically and gradually disappearing from the scene. On the other side, I still kept standing on the same place.

Chapter 3
Agony is inevitable

Unable to spend time together from so many days (and also leaving our 'day meeting' incomplete), on the evening of 19th of February we both decided to meet at 'Isla Moon', a garden restaurant located at the outskirts of city. I had never seen such a restaurant before. It has such a serene ambience due to its lit-up gazebos, soft flute music, and a small pond with lotuses and milky white ducks. I saw Ranil already waiting for me in one of the gazebos. When he saw me entering, he stood up and started glowing surrounded by those wonderful lamps. With his formals on, it seemed like he had come for a proper romantic date; whereas I was simply dressed in ice-blue shaded jeans and a white t-shirt.

"You are looking beautiful." Gazing at me with his twinkling eyes Ranil whispered in my ears. I felt a tingling sensation when he did that. Shyly stepping back, I double-checked myself to confirm if I was actually looking pretty?

"I hope I am not late" I said with a quivering voice. He smirked and swept aside my full fringe with his hands. "Now they look perfect, Okay! Come, let us sit here." He spoke without a break, pointing towards a purple-coloured couch. Making myself comfortable on the squishy seat, I uttered- "Shirley dropped me here, but she won't be coming to pick me up. Will you drop me to her home?"

"Ruhani! Is this a question to be asked? Of course, I will. But why not your home?"

"No! I mean, I will stay at Shirley's home tonight."

"Oh, fine. So, tell me, how's the preparation for the exam going?"

"Ranil! I think this is a date! Isn't it?"

"You know it very well; I cannot initiate a romantic conversation. That's your job!" he laughed saying this.

"Ranil....I will miss you." Looking into his eyes I spoke with a tear twinkling in my eye. "I don't know why I chose you? Who are you to me?" I hushed.

"Your Eternal love!" he said. Then, looking aside he started singing,

"Mera pyaar wo hai ke markar tumko, juda apni baahon se hone na dega."

I was enraptured by his voice and lyrics of the song.

"I never heard this song before, but I must say, it is very melodious."

"Yeah, it became more melodious when I sang it for you, hehehe."

"Ranil, your school life is going to end after a few days. You will be in college with some new dreams, new hopes and obviously new friends. I am not insecure, but what if someone else grabs your attention. Will you give my crown to her?"

Hearing my words, Ranil held my hand and said, "Listen Ruhani, you don't need to think so much. I can understand your concern, but trust me, you hold a unique position in my life. With you, I feel so positive; such a vibrant personality you possess! I can never dim the light of your love, understood?"

I nodded my head and embraced him, feeling proud that I gave this gentle guy a special space in my life.

The more time we spent together, the more we were getting addicted to each other. Ranil always exposed his harsh side sometimes by making me see the realities of life. The talks of separation, different background, families and obligations always came in our way to see the future together, and he repeated these words often.

"I want to tell you something if you don't mind?" asked Anjali politely.

"Yeah sure."

"If Ranil was so indecisive, then why did you decide to marry him only? Generally, a man can love you with all his heart. However, if the question of future makes his blood run cold, it's time to think again- 'Is he *really* the one?' Only a strong headed and decisive man can hold your hand forever, crossing all obstacles; and if a person truly loves you, he will. There is no place for excuses. Though I can understand Ranil was a teenager at that time, but some traits are carried forward." Completing her sentence Anjali looked at Ruhani, expecting her to understand this simple concept.

Ruhani flashed a grin and replied, "Just like you, Shirley too was my guide in the matter of my relationship with Ranil. She would give me so much advice. Though Ranil didn't like it, it was the only thing of mine which he disliked; and let me tell you, he won't like your advice to me too."

"Don't take it otherwise, dear. I know he is your husband, as you mentioned. I was merely disclosing a fact." Smiling mildly, Anjali spoke without any regret about sharing her opinion.

"Hmm… I understand. Actually, he wanted our relationship to be totally private. No photographs together, no meetings outside the school, nothing. Just he and me, and only his best friend knew about us. However, I didn't have any problem sharing the news that we are together with all my close ones; except his 'talks about consequences' I never shared anything 'personal' with them.

Ranil was unaware that Shirley was his shadow who always insisted me to be practical. She once said- "Listen Ruhani, this is a teenage love; just enjoy it to that extent. No one can anticipate the future. You never know what personality Ranil would possess attaining the age of maturity; will your nature go in tandem with his? You never know! Future is uncertain. I advise you not to think about the future. Just cherish your present moments with him, that's it. And you should not forget, you are engaged."

The words of me 'being engaged' always agitated me. "Don't you dare to say that I am engaged." I shouted at Shirley, as I didn't want anyone to remind me of that unfortunate incident.

"Fine, I won't; but don't go deep into these feelings with Ranil. It's a myth that you can't live without a person. Don't make yourself vulnerable; protect your soul from being naked in front of him."

"Then why should I walk on the path which is uncertain and temporary?" I asked befuddled.

"Only because you love each other so much. It's true Ruhani; I have never witnessed a couple like you who talks so much, has zero insecurity about each other, and does no show-off of their love. You both are happy in your own way. I truly wish everything goes well for you. But if everything happens contradictory to what you are thinking, don't choose the path of self-destruction. Are you understanding? Most importantly you both are still nibba nibbi, hehe… so don't think too much."

"Shut up Shirley!" I pushed her slightly and smiled, but I wasn't ready to accept those heavy words. I wanted to be with Ranil forever, without even imagining a separation from him.

Those days were remarkable. We were creating enrapturing moments together. He once told me that he had never met someone like me, and will never, even after his marriage, be able to forget me. Yeah, his marriage!! How could he even think of being with married to someone else when I was walking beside him?! Those words of his pushed me to the edge. I got the hint that though he loves me immensely, he didn't hold the valour to make me his queen. I knew that it was too early to think about our marriage, but perhaps in my deliberation to escape my forced engagement, I was desperate to have a future with Ranil.

However, even as I started dreaming about marriage with Ranil, I was aware that the track that I was opting for, was thorny. I always thought- "To turn my reverie into reality I need to do something really big", but I knew Ranil had different views. He was a very practical person. We both were on the same track, thinking about an uncertain future. The only difference was that I had a positive approach and he clutched to a negative one.

*

In the month of March, I had my board examinations. That time, the CCE pattern gave an alternative to the students of class 10th, to either go for central board or home board. The exams of the students who opted for central board were conducted in different schools, and for home board students their own school was their examination centre. Shirley and I chose the 'home board' option. For Ranil, appearing in central board was obligatory as he was in 12th grade.

Three students of my class who had their roll numbers between mine and Shirley, opted for central board. Consequently, it brought Shirley's roll number next to mine. It made Shirley sanguine about her examination performance. She was in high spirits thinking about me sitting right in front of her during exams.

The day before our first exam Shirley rang and psyched me up for the exams. At last, she came to the main point- "Ruhani, I have not covered the whole syllabus. Please do show me the answers tomorrow; you know I don't like science much" she begged.

"Shirley, you are my best friend, don't worry, I will tell you all the answers" I assured her.

She was on cloud nine with my assurance. In the morning, all students were assembled in the school ground. Our Vice principal gave us a motivational speech and announced the examination hall numbers allotted to the roll numbers. Shirley and I were allotted in the same hall. The invigilator commanded each of us to check one's seat number (written on a small sheet which was pasted on the door) before entering the room. My seat number was 30 and Shirley's was 31. She was all set to cheat in the exam. We entered the room and started searching the seats allotted to us. We both saw seat no. 30 together. Shirley stopped dead in tracks. Her face grew pale. She had become a hapless victim of the sitting arrangement. Seat no. 30 was the last seat of 3rd row and seat no. 31 was the front seat of 4th row!

"Ruhani! I was totally dependent on you. Now how will you show me all the answers?" she wailed, slapping her forehead in tension.

"Shirley, don't worry. Haven't you studied anything?"

"I did...but... Ruhani, quickly give me brief overview of all the chapters."

"Okay... still there are 15 minutes left... listen...." I gave her a quick overview of all the chapters.

The final bell rang, alerting us all for the beginning of the exam. Students started chanting God's name for the last time. The invigilator started distributing the answer sheets and question papers. I read the question paper thoroughly and started writing the answers. Suddenly I noticed Shirley looking at me feebly from the first bench. I wanted to condole with her in her extremity but I quickly re-focussed on answer writing.

"What are you doing? What do you think, the examiner is a nincompoop?" shouted the invigilator. I looked up to see to who he was scolding. Obviously - it was Shirley.

"No sir, I haven't done anything," Shirley spoke meekly.

"Don't try to fool me. Are you not showing your answers to the girl sitting behind you? Tell me."

"Hainn... What? Am I?" Shirley was at sea listening to his words. She herself didn't know a single answer, but gently apologised so as to stop the storm in a teacup.

From that day, Shirley decided not to be over-reliant on anyone. It was best decision she ever took!

I scored 9.5 CGPA in class 10[th,] Shirley's performance was good in all subjects except science. Her D2 grade in that subject was offending her eyes. Soon the result of class 12th was also announced. Ranil had scored 80%. I, Ranil and Shirley decided to give ourself a small party, albeit, the money came out only from Ranil's pocket, hahahaha!"

"Wow...So you both enjoyed so many years of relationship. That's great" Anjali exclaimed in excitement.

"We never." answered Ruhani losing herself in the woods, where she was accompanied by loneliness.

"What? Never!" Anjali squealed, disbelieving Ruhani.

"Yes, as I told you earlier, he was my senior and it was his last year in the school. It was obvious for him to go, but he went without uttering a single word. He vanished as if he never existed." Without blinking her eyes, Ruhani replied in a soft tone, looking at the wall steadily.

"Gone!!!" Unable to understand a sudden change Anjali experienced a shock. "But where? How did it happen?"

"The last thing was an eye contact, I remember that. After that, he just vanished from my life. I read his eyes; they revealed everything what he felt for me. It was excruciating period. He was out of my contact; his Facebook account was deactivated. Yet, I tried to search him at every possible place. I asked about him indirectly to his cousin and everyone who knew him, but unfortunately, I wasn't that close to anyone of them to ask everything clearly. Meera told me once that he was in Bangalore.

'Did he ever love me?' I wondered. Those sweet little signs were scanty to trace that he truly felt for me. Shirley was right. None of us possess static personalities; people alter with time.

He was so good to me, why did he leave me like this? Was I over-thinking? He never promised me anything. Then, why did I cling to fashioned dreams of togetherness on basis of hypothesis? The cyclone of questions surrounded me, creating high and low pressure in my mind."

Anjali was sitting wordlessly beside Ruhani, feeling each and every of her emotion. What was she supposed to speak now rather than letting the woman continue the story of her catastrophe?!

"Shirley urged me to forget him. She kept telling me, "Ruhani, he might have found someone for him. He resides in Bangalore; he is such a practical person. It is your stupidity to think that he is still into you" she would say, and advise me to focus on my studies as Class 11th was a crucial stage. But any kind of motivational words were useless for me. Shirley's long lectures to pull me out of that emotional burden never yielded lucrative results. Her long and motivational lectures seemed to me as the words from a witch!

I am mindful of the fact that on one Saturday she visited me with some impulse videos of influencers on YouTube. Grinning like a Cheshire cat I welcomed her, since my parents were out. We made ourselves comfortable in the living room. Sitting on the sofa, Shirley rummaged through her purse and took out a Cadbury Dairy Milk Silk. Though that chocolate always makes my heart leap, but that time it failed to do so.

"Thank you, Shirley; but I won't eat this much. Let's share."

"Ruhani! Are you serious? This is Dairy Milk! You are that girl who never leaves a single piece of this chocolate for anyone. I can't understand this sacrifice!" She was shocked to see my changed behaviour.

"Shirley, leave this. Tell me the reason behind your presence?"

"Here, hold this." She spoke handing over her mobile to me. "Here are some videos; I have only downloaded them for you." Yeah, downloading was a big thing during those days, we didn't have any 4G or 5G. Hardly she knew that those videos were a kind of dross to me.

Making me watch each one of it and later rationalizing it all, she once again invested her time to save her friend from mental illness. She was unknown of the fact that the time she invested was a complete wastage, because I was not ready to understand anything. After a while I looked at Shirley and smirked at her concern. She probably noticed my insolent act; her sullen face gave me hint of her wounded heart.

"Shirley, you are just burning daylight here. Better you save your energy for some productive things; my mind isn't ready to accept anything currently. You may leave now." I knew very well that those words would have hurt her, but I blurted those words somehow with a bleeding heart. Her face blackened even more listening to my harsh words. Hopelessly looking at me, she walked straight towards the exit. Gulping saliva, I followed her quietly, feeling very guilty for whatever I spoke.

"Bye" she said with a straight face.

But I could see that she knew her friend and her current condition very well. She saw my moist eyes looking at her vulnerably. "You are an idiot!" Shirley said and embraced me. Keeping my head on her shoulder I snivelled uncontrollably over my condition for which only 'I' was responsible.

"Don't cry Ruhani, you will be fine soon; everything will change. This is just a phase, strive to come out of it. And I know, one day you will." She spoke caressing my head. "I should leave now." Saying this she sat on her scooter and left me in that hollow house all alone.

She never visited my home again. School was the only place where I got to see her, though we did keep having long telephonic conversations. Unfortunately trapped by the angel of darkness, acting in contrast to my personality, throwing the world's most malapert remarks, especially on Shirley, became my habit. That colleen condoned my cold side illimitably. But there is a limit to taking your close ones for granted; I was impotent to understand this simple thing. As time passed, Shirley's name popping up on my screen also started becoming a rare occurrence. Who could blame her?!

I knew my negative vibes would have affected her heavily. There is limit to handle a toxic person who doesn't want to change. Yet, instead of talking to her face-to-face for sorting out the growing differences between us, I kept my ego as first preference. Distancing myself from Shirley was a Himalayan blunder, but she never left my side completely.

Apart from being brash, an additional witless habit that I adopted was mailing Ranil on a daily basis. I kept him up-to-date about my emotional turbulence, as well as, with the hell that I was going through. I wasn't sure whether he was reading my mails or not, but there was not a single day when I didn't mail him. In expectation of getting a single reply, I kept mailing him for years. I was not ready to accept that he had left me without speaking a single word. I was preparing myself to move on. It was easy to say but onerous, too onerous, to implement. I wanted to linger over him, and only him.

My mental condition was deteriorating day by day. I was unable to focus on my studies anymore. I started isolating myself from everyone and lost my geniality. People started describing me as cantankerous person; it became my key nature.

Nightmares about me and Ranil getting apart always horrified me. I spent many hours of darkness shedding tears in distress for him. I hid my condition from everyone; I was living two different lives with two different Ruhanis. Later, my exam results exposed my duality. The result bothered my parents a lot. They asked me the reason behind my odd behaviour, but I was disinterested in telling them anything.

One of our very generous and affable neighbours suggested them to take me to a psychiatrist, but my parents confuted his standpoint by saying that their daughter is not barmy.

Shirley again urged me to focus on my studies as it was the last year of school. Rohit too became worried when he got to know my 11th standard result.

"Rohit? Who was he?" asked Anjali.

"A friend from coaching institute. We were not close friends, we just exchanged notes. That's it. But he was an empath, for sure. Consoling me, he always said, 'Ruhani dear, I can understand your condition, but don't do this to yourself. If Ranil would have been present here, he would have definitely scolded you. Trust me Ruhani, don't take load thinking about him. God is planning something grand for you'.

And I had same reply. 'Rohit, can you do same with the girl who you love?' I would counter-question him like a needy person ravenous for love.

Shirley didn't want me to ruin my life thinking about Ranil anymore. She would keep explaining that he does not belong to the people I belong to; he is from different sect which is antithetical to my religious beliefs. It was beyond the bounds of possibility for both of us to live with each other. By chance if we create a medley of two different cultures, this society would mould the story and give it a hideous face making it onerous for both of us to survive together. I would nod my head in front of her, but in reality, her words were strangling me.

I know she was delivering all those words for my well-being, but I was stuck. For me Ranil getting faded from my life brought back the horrifying reality of my engagement. I saw him as the one who would take me away from my worst nightmare, but I never anticipated he would give me the same. I was mistaken to see him as my saviour.

Ruhani's vulnerability was giving Anjali mixed feelings. At one point she was thinking 'How could a lady destruct herself like this in spite of seeing the reality?' Yet, at the back of her mind Anjali also had another thought: 'It's not her mistake, she was moulded by this society to think in that way, more emotionally rather than intelligently.' Blinking her eyes, she spoke- "Ruhani, sometimes lack of courage throws us into making blunders. I don't blame you; you were a mere child who was given irrelevant nightmare by her own parents. But at this point of time, I want to say, no one will come to save you. It is only you, your own internal strength, and hopeful voice who can do that."

"I understand whatever you are saying; but implementing it is so difficult. The only inner voice I have been trusting so far has been a negative one, because I have only seen negative incidents happen in reality. There has only been pain in my life. How can such a person even imagine something good happening with them? I have never been so lucky" sighed Ruhani.

"Well, how can you hope for a mermaid when you yourself are raising an evil shark?" Anjali asked her with a smile.

"What do you mean?" asked Ruhani seeking for clarity.

"Oh, nothing, but you were really lucky to have friend like Shirley beside you."

"Yeah, I was. She was always ready to help with her lectures. She rebuffed the fact of 'Ranil's feeling for me', I expostulated with her on this, giving her instances of Ranil's love for me. Ultimately, I found myself in a predicament because my arguments in connection with speaking in favour of Ranil's feelings were conjecture. I wanted to dump every thought of Ranil. Facts that once indicated that he loved me, were not convincing me to retain his memories anymore. Alas, whenever I decided to throw Ranil out from my mind, tragically it always resulted in one more vain attempt. I was still twitterpated over his love. Considering it as my destiny to live without him, I made my pillowcase wet every night. My silent cry sometimes jinxed Ranil which eventually turned into self-torment.

Knock Knock. "May I ladies?" asked Mr Singh.

"Hello sir..." wished Anjali.

"So how are you, Miss Ruhani? Feeling better now?" he asked.

"Yes sir."

As soon as Ruhani finished speaking, Anjali looked at Mr Singh and told him to come with her. Both of them came out of the room.

"Did she tell you something important?" asked the cop.

"Well, I am trying to know about her and her condition, but it will take time. I think she is too sensitive to be handled by you" Anjali said with a smile.

 Mr Singh laughed, "Ok Anjali, I will come again. Hope the whole matter would be laid bare before you soon." Anjali assured Mr Singh and went back into the room. "Huhhhhhh...So Ruhani.... What happened next? Did someone else fill the void left by Ranil?"

"No, I never allowed anyone to do that. Any boy who thought about me seemed to me like a demon who came into my life to peter out all the memories pertaining to Ranil. I maintained distance from them. I know I was wrong; I should have moved on. But my heart never permitted me. Memories of Ranil were making me frail, my mind and body were experiencing catastrophic changes. It was vacuous of me to destroy myself massively. In this whole scenario, I forgot about the one with whom I was forcefully engaged. Hahaha, well it was good to not remember him."

"But Ruhani, you were too young to think like that. Even when you grow older, you should never punish yourself by waiting for someone who never cared about you. Be with the one who actually wants to be with you, who wants to spend his life with you" advised Anjali, making her understand the meaning of being alive.

"Sister, Ranil is my husband now, don't forget. But if you are telling me this thing in relation to those days, then yes, I agree I was living with an erroneous belief that time. But as I told you earlier, my heart was not permitting me. Somewhere it kept the hope alive that one day he will come back.

Time was moving on, but the one for whom I whimpered every night never returned. In the devilish dark I was lulled by his memories which acted as cool moonlight - shiny and pacific. His memories were static, stationary, immovable. That thing made me suffer from depression. My eyes were always filled up with tears. "The person for who I am pining away, will never know my agony." That was the only thought stuck in my mind. My parents became concerned about my condition; they wanted me to get out of this hell. Breaking their stereotypical mindset, they finally decided to take me to a psychiatrist. I was not ready for any therapy because I wanted to be in pain. I don't know why; but the idea of being happy terrified me!

I was taken to Dr Sunil Mathur's clinic; he was a well-known psychiatrist. He showed me some random pictures of abstract art and told me to depict all the images. I did, and then he asked me the reason for feeling horrendous and restless every time. I was speechless. The lack of hardihood in my personality resisted me from speaking up about Ranil in front of my parents. I blamed the pressure of board examinations for my condition. He gave me medicines which acted on my mind in an anomalous way, I started behaving like a fatuous teenager or as if I was a 10 or 11-year-old girl. The people who tagged me as an eminent girl started calling me a nutcase behind my back. The people who I once called my friends turned their faces away from me when I needed them the most. My own relatives mocked me. That day I realized that having enemies is better than feeding snake-faced people. Shirley felt bad for me. She always saw me as a girl whose versatility became her identity and made her popular in the school but was now left all alone with a mental illness.

Eliminating the spaces which I created between me and Shirley, one day I went to her residence. Holding a hot cup of coffee, I confessed to her that I wanted to quit. For me, tackling the pressure of grade 12th was becoming next to impossible, but more than that, I had a fear of scoring low as I always maintained my image as a coruscating student. Sensing my anxiety, Shirley reacted in the same way that I thought she would.

"Yes Ruhani, your decision is scrupulous, go for it. But after few years if you see your classmates making large of their life and beaming with pride, then please don't feel contrite about your decision." Shirley's words forced me to think about the puerile act I was ready to do.

"What are you up to, Ruhani? All your cousin sisters were married at the age of 14. You were fortunate that God wrote a rose-coloured destiny for you. At this point you are not just lessening your sangfroid but you are doubting God's plans too. Don't do this.

No one can enlighten you in this world except you yourself. The people who care for you will stand by your side in the tempest but they can't do anything more than that. You are the one who will have to take actions."

Shirley tried her best to bring me back on the track. Consequently, instead of giving up studies I quitted the idea of quitting it. But I chose a second option, which was 'escapism'. I had my sleeping pills to help me achieve that. I found solace in slumbering for hours. I didn't want to come back to reality. I stopped attending school, skipped my half-yearly exams and unit tests. Shilly-shallying, collywobbles became my partner in loneliness. Fear to face people and their questions forced me to imprison myself in a room. I was shattered; my own behaviour bedimmed all hopes I had regarding my future. Everything was blurred, everything. Ruhani who knew the language of patience and hope was vanquished by the Ruhani who was captured by the fiends of hell.

In spite of getting everyone's motivation, my class 12th outcome proved to be mediocre. I passed my 12th board exams but not with great grades. My parents were not pleased with my performance, nor was I. It made me feel guilty because I was the reason behind their gloomy faces. Anyhow, my father managed to get me admission in one of the first-rated college of the city.

Noticing no change in me, my father decided to switch my psychiatrist.

Chapter 4
Aurora behind the curtains

My friend Rohit recommended Dr Ozil's name. Ozil was Rohit's cousin, and was new in this profession. Looking at my parents' faces who hankered to bring their cheerful daughter back to her glorious life, I agreed to go for the treatment. We arrived at the given address; my father stopped the car in front of the clinic named 'Ozil's Therapies'. We entered the clinic where a beautiful girl looked at me. "Hello miss, do you have any appointment?" she asked.

"Yes, yes; we do." My father replied. I was standing in silence beside him, full of fear. My personality suffered a lot during those days; being timorous and sad had become the chief characteristics of my nature. The receptionist sensed who the patient was.

"Take this. It is your token number. Till then please be comfortable in waiting area" she spoke with a smiling face.

"Thank you." said my father. We entered in. I saw the steel chairs attached to each other and placed in a sequence. On the right side of the door was a book shelf with some magazines and newspapers kept in it. The people sitting there started looking at us. My father made me sit down on one of the chairs. My pale face and tired eyes were a hint enough that I was the patient.

I saw a man in his 30s staring at me. I too started staring at him. He found it awkward and turned his eyes towards another woman. I also noticed a couple who was sitting beside me with an old woman, whispering- "this girl is so young but demented. Such a pity."

"I felt bad. It was depression. I was not a demented case. Why do people consider mental disease as a taboo? And that too especially those people who were sitting there for their own case! Hypocrites! I thought…"

"Miss Ruhani" the receptionist called out. We three stood up and went out from the waiting room. She showed us the way to Dr. Ozil's room. The moment I took my first step in the room, he gave me a pointed look. His room was a calm place and, I can still recall the soulful melodies being played in the background.

He offered me seat and asked my father about my behavioural pattern. One by one my father started mentioning the facts of my unusual behaviour. Dr was listening to my case very calmly. He was a young and personable professional. After talking to my father, he expressed a desire to talk to me alone. He requested my parents to wait outside. When my parents headed towards the exit, I kept looking at them like a nursery class kid who looks at her parents when they leave her all alone in a new school.

"Ahem, Ahem, hey hello ma'am." Dr greeted me.

"Hello" I said.

"So, what happened? What's killing you inside? Tell me clearly. I am here to understand you. You don't need to create any boundaries. Be free to speak." He spoke with a smiling face. I was quite as I was not willing to answer him anything.

"Oh, so you don't want to speak anything." Saying this, he waited for me to reply, but I was still quiet. "Okay.... fine." He continued- "Let me tell you a small conversation between Akbar and Birbal."

"Ahem, ahem." Adjusting his voice tone and making it slightly heavy Ozil spoke. "One day, Akbar said to Birbal – *"Birbal humein ek aisi pankti sunao jise koi khushi mai padhe to gham haasil ho, aur gham mai padhe toh khushi haasil ho'.* (Birbal, tell me a sentence which if people hear in happiness, they feel sad; and if they hear in sadness, they feel happy.)

Listening to the king's request, Birbal replied- 'Ye waqt guzar jaayega.' (This time shall also pass.)

Hearing him, I looked up at the kind Doctor with tears in my eyes. I started crying and opened the book of my dolour. My wet eyes revealed everything to him; he was listening to me with deep concern. It was for the first time when I actually felt someone trying his best to figure out my problems. Well, sure, it was his job, but the earnestness with which he did it made my heavy heart feel lighter. Dr. Ozil looked into my eyes and advised me not to overstretch my ordeal. He gave me a list of medicines and told me to visit again after a week.

The day he called me was a Sunday. I went to his clinic, but it was closed. I cursed Ozil for his disappearance. His absence vexed me. I was about to reverse my steps but suddenly a voice stopped me calling from back. It was Dr Ozil. "Hello doctor" I greeted him.

"Hello Ruhani, how are you now? Are the medicines working well?" he asked.

I simply nodded my head, as I was annoyed at him.

"Why have you called me today? Your clinic is closed, isn't it?" I asked.

"Yes, it is, but my real job is outside this clinic." Dr said. "If you don't mind can I take you out for a coffee?" he added. Without thinking much, I said yes and sat in his car. He took me to a small cafe with just one waiter on duty. We sat in the corner seat and he started telling me about his life.

"I am a doctor by profession, but in reality, I am just like you. I too come in a category of heartbroken people" he revealed, taking a sip of hot coffee.

"Were you also left adrift by a person without any last words?"

"Yes, it has happened with me. I too was left by a beautiful lady - Charu, the woman of my dream." His voice quivered speaking this. I saw a tear twinkling in his eyes but he resisted from letting it stream down.

"Why did she leave you, sir?"

"She didn't want to, but she had to."

"Why? Was it due to family pressure?"

"No dear. God was reason behind it. He snatched her from me 3 years back. What a lady she was!" Ozil spoke in quivery voice. He was so entranced talking about his lady love Charulika, that he didn't care about noticing the reaction of the listener. Suddenly, Dr. Ozil asked, "Will you allow me to take to you to my home?" His words shook me. 'What does he want? What are his intentions?' I thought.

"Trust me Ruhani, there is no harm" he said, as if reading my mind. His words had a sense of assurance which made me count on him, and I agreed. He told me to sit in his car, the way to his home was not much far from the cafe. We soon reached his home. Watching the car come near to the house, the watchman rushed to open the main gate. Ozil drove the car in slowly.

He stopped the car, stepped out and came to my side. Opening car's gate for me, slightly bending his back, he spoke gently - "Here is the destination ma'am." Stepping out, I saw a beautifully constructed house decorated with red roses, highlighted by white background of the building. I looked at Ozil with amazement. "Don't look at me like this, it's not done by me. My father is the sole creator of this empyrean; but five years ago, I lost him too."

I shook my head and turned my face away.

Another watchman came running and handed Ozil the keys. Unlocking the door, he paved the way for me. As soon as I entered inside, my eyes confronted the alluring golden lights, golden wallpapers, and the deep black coloured statues. Al of this seemed to have a hypnotizing effect on my eyes. Taking small steps and watching everything keenly I reached a life-sized hall, where I saw pictures of Dr Ozil hanging on each and every wall. "Maybe he is a self-obsessed person," I thought.

I was looking at the pictures with all my focus. My eyes were rolling across the walls without a hiatus, but eventually they were halted by something unusual. I saw something peculiar. In front of me was a portrait hanging on the wall. It was of a lady; she was posing in royal posture and in traditional attire. I was confused. To some extent the features and physique of the lady were matching with mine. "I shouldn't have trusted this Doctor" I thought. I again became sceptical about his intentions. Ozil sensed what I was thinking. He was smiling at me and slowly came close, whispering. "That is Charulika."

Yes, the woman looked like me! Her eyes, her lips, that face cut were similar to mine. I thought the Doctor was mistaken for considering me as her; I was not his better half. Mystified, I gave him a callous look; my eyes grew big in anger. Murmuring, I started heading towards the door. Following me he gripped my hand from behind. I quickly swiped his hand to unclasp mine. Taking fast steps with a restless heart I turned around begging Ozil to let me go. But, once again he clasped my hand, and this time tighter.

"Keep calm, keep calm Ruhani." He spoke softly. "Relax your mind" he requested. Holding my hand, he took me back to the hall. Making me sit comfortably he handed me a glass of water and started pouring out his words. He pattered, he babbled, we discussed. Uncovering all his wounds he spoke in a manner that I felt connected and was able to relate to everything.

I looked into his eyes; they were true. Ranil used to say, I possess a special quality of reading people's eyes to know their soul. I don't know whether these lines are false or a real fact.

That whole day Ozil talked to me. He galvanized me for bringing about change in myself. His constructive words began affecting my mind in a positive way. From that Sunday, my every day was spent with him. He told me wondrous things which should be followed in the journey of life. He displayed to me different pictures of this world. His positive persona and success stories had a stimulating effect on me. My gradual transformation made me believe in energies, his positive energy started overriding my negative ones. He introduced me to a universe I was unaware of. I started admiring him. He made me learn 'not to be self-destructible'.

Charu was his favourite topic. His elation would peak whenever he talked about her, but in tandem with that, I would notice the accumulated grief in his heart. Every word he spoke about Charulika would reveal how much he was attached to her. Ozil told me everything about him and Charulika. The woman was a true angel. She was a social worker, who looked for love in eyes of orphanages and abandoned elders. Talking with him alleviated my suffering; I was in need of a person like Ozil.

With passing time, Dr Ozil carved a special place in my life. Many people took it in the wrong way, but we had a healthy relation.

One day, Ozil and I were sitting on the banks of a lake. I looked at him and said - Don't worry sir, you deserve a dazzling future. Miracles do exist. You should try to move on, there is no age for falling in love." Hearing this, Ozil gave me a weird look. I kept waiting for him to reply. Instead, his questioning eyes were looking at me as if my words sounded unpleasant to him. At long last, he smiled and spoke only three words – "Why don't you?" Saying this, he stood up and left me alone. His small sentence forced me to mull over my situation. It was his job to make a person realize about the right things for him/her. From so many days I was thinking that this man still walks with past memories of his gone wife. I thought he was a hypocrite, as he didn't seem to practice what he preached. However, I never assumed that the person was trying to make me see things from his perspective, where I was able to distinguish between right and wrong. What was I doing with my life? I was destroying myself for the person who never felt any need to know whether I was alive or dead. That day I promised myself to alter my personality from downbeat to bubbly. It was the initial stage of beginning to forget a baseless past.

From that day on, I started living my life without any worries. 'If something is meant to happen, it will' became the theme of my life. I was finally learning to love myself. I was glittering, laughing and trying to invigorate all those relations which had become decayed in the interim. My self-confidence started blooming; I was back with a bang. 'Ruhani' once more became a known name among people. Though Ranil's memories were still in my heart, but now the mode of living with those memories was changed. My perception about love was transformed. I started realizing that it is not mandatory to spend your life with the person you love. Love is when we wish that the person remains happy wherever he is. I recognised my feelings as one-sided and wished the best for Ranil, though I found I wasn't able to overcome from it wholly. Even Ozil was unaware about my stuck condition, because I was totally fine, living my life.

In this way, three years passed like a dew rolling down from the rose petal.

One rainy night, lying on the bed with earphones stuck in my ears, I was listening to the song-

Dil mai sanam ki soorat,

aankhon mai aashique de

mere khuda mujhe tu

ek aur zindagi de.

Closing my eyes, I travelled back to the years when Ranil was with me. Suddenly I felt a vibration. It was my phone ringing. I looked at its screen, the caller was the only non-blood relative of mine who had stood beside me during my horrifying period, in spite of my churlishness.

"Hello Shirley." I spoke running towards the window, keeping my voice low.

"Hello Ruhani, how are you?"

"I am fine. How are you?"

"Don't ask dear, just went through latest crush breakup."

"Thank god it's only a crush breakup, it's good that you never fell in love with anyone." I still don't know why I was telling her so. I think that time I became weak enough to support the feeling called 'love'.

"Ruhani, why you think like that? You can't blame love for all the miseries people face when they fall for someone. You have lost your strength to love someone again. Don't do this. Be strong to hold the hand of the person who cares for you, just like Doctor Ozil."

"Shut up Shirley. Dr and I are good friends. Please change your perception" I shouted in agitation.

"Whatever. It was a simple suggestion. Ranil has become the talk of the past" she said, not aware how strenuous it was for me to feel the same way for someone, as I felt for Ranil. Ranil's each and everything was flawless for me, but it never happened in case of others who tried to become a part of my life. But it is a best friend's job to make us understand each and everything forcibly, even though we don't want to. Our chat was humorous, serious and long. We both were laughing at our lives and situations. At the end she added that the exam enrolment card of the final year was out. That statement alarmed my mind.

"No more imagination and magical world, my dear. Reality has come to test you" I told myself and started preparing for giving my best shot.

<h1 style="text-align:center">Chapter 5</h1>

<h2 style="text-align:center">Life takes turn in an unexpected way</h2>

Finally, exams arrived and dried up the throat of each and every student. It was the first day of examination. Students started streaming in to the examination hall, nervousness writ large on their faces. The invigilator's voice of echoed in the hall like a lion roaring in the woods, but we students were not meek deer. We all were like soldiers who had entered a battlefield with a resolution to fight the battle with great gusto. There I suddenly saw a familiar face; she was Ranil's cousin. I walked towards her to ask a barrage of questions about Ranil; but then, I stopped myself midway. With wet eyes I sat on my seat looking at her constantly. After writing my exam, I didn't even wait for Shirley. I just rushed home and turned on my laptop to see Ranil. I had huge collection of Ranil's photographs, secretly kept in a folder named 'error'. My tears were proof that I was unable to stop his memories from scratching my heart, but now I was also aware of other worldly things. Shutting off the laptop, I opened my books for the next paper. I studied aggressively, vigorously; I knew it would be a change-maker in my static life.

Like every start has its end, our exams too reached its last phase of sitting with relaxation and waiting for the results. Within one month the result of my performance was on my computer screen. It showered me with happiness as I had passed the exams with good grades. I applied for a scholarship and hostel facility in one of the renowned colleges of the capital city of our state. My father agreed to send me to a different city as he wanted me to prepare for the civil services competition exam.

I was over the moon due to crossing the cut-off which approved the application of my scholarship, as well as, of the hostel. First thing I did listening to this good news was mailing Ranil. I was rejoicing those moments with my family and friends, only one person was missing in that celebration - Dr. Ozil. I picked up my phone and opened my call list to call him but suddenly my phone buzzed. The caller was 'Ozil' itself! "Long live Ozil" I spoke and attended the call.

"Hello."

"Hello" I replied, "Who is this, and where is Dr Ozil?" I asked, because the voice sounded unfamiliar.

"Ma'am, actually we have found a man here. He has been taken out from the Kaylana lake. We found this phone lying on the banks. We are taking him to the City Hospital, please come fast."

Listening to those words my heart started throbbed expeditiously. It felt leaden with the pain of losing someone very precious to me again. My hands were shivering; I was unable to reply. "The one who made me brave enough to live, himself turned to be such a weak person?" I thought.

Everyone was waiting for me outside my room. I rushed out; seeing the colour drained from my face made everyone alert of something bad having happened. "What happened Ruhani? Why are you looking so stricken?" asked my father. I looked at him and somehow mustered strength to inform everyone about Ozil - "I don't know whether he is alive or not, they took him to the City Hospital" I spoke shivering. But, surprisingly, none of them gave a shocked reaction to this ghastly news! They started taking it as a joke.

"Please Ruhani, enough of your jokes" my mother said with a smile.

"This is not a joke!" I yelled. "Ozil is in critical condition." My frantic yelling turned the joyous scene sombre. Noticing my grievous face everyone realized the seriousness of my words. We all rushed to the hospital. Reaching there, I heard the ambulance roaring with its sirens. That sound horrified me. My heart was throbbing fast, I was praying for Ozil being optimistic about his well-being but at the same time I was in fear of losing a dear friend. We ran towards the reception desk. The receptionist looked at me but I was unable to ask anything. My father, who was standing behind, hastily came forward and asked the receptionist about Ozil.

"Are you enquiring about the man who attempted suicide?"

We nodded our head.

"He has been shifted from the emergency ward to the ICU" she informed.

We all rushed to the ICU. I was in so much trauma that I tried to enter inside. I became obstreperous; like a savage animal, I was hitting everyone who tried to stop me from entering in. At last, my parents controlled me somehow. But the matter didn't end there. Now, my mind started visualizing everything happening inside the ICU. In my imagination which was more inclined towards negative thoughts, I saw Ozil striving to breath and the doctors striving hard to help him breath. I paused my imagination and began strengthening myself to get to grips with the lamentable situation which could be the consequence of Ozil's pusillanimous act. That living soul, with whom I was so much attached, was on the wane. It was an excruciating time for me. Attachment is hell, attachment is pain. I felt that heartbreak once again; my angel was struggling to survive. I again started delving about the things happening inside ICU. 'The medical staff must be preparing themselves to give him an electric shock on the chest. Will it be their last try, their last hope?' I wondered. The doctor must have placed the defibrillators on his chest, making his body jerk again, and again, and again. All the time I was on tenterhooks to know the final condition of my friend. Suddenly, the doctor came out of the ICU. I rushed to ask him about Ozil's condition. The doctor gave us a bleak look which was enough to make me realise what he wanted to unveil. I stopped him from speaking anything as I lacked the lion-heartedness which was needed to hear the petrifying words. I was not so strong to see my friend lying lifeless on that bed. Rohit, his only cousin, started sobbing loudly. My parents tried to pacify him, but I was standing still. Ozil's lifeless body was ready to be taken out of the room but was I ready to see it? No, I was not. As if on auto-cue, I walked out from the hospital, hired a taxi and went to my home. All the way, I kept thinking about the reason behind Ozil's unexpected act. I was startled but everyone was in shock pondering about the reason behind a very unlikely suicide. The man who knew only one formula i.e., 'live and let live', how could he become self-destructive like this? Was the situation so ominous that it made person like him lily-livered?

Ozil's body was taken for post-mortem. Police were inquiring everything about him from everyone who knew him. They informed us about his suicide letter, asking the reasons which could have made him take his life. I don't know if they found any evidence or not. After the post mortem, his body was given to us for cremation. Unfortunately, Ozil's relatives didn't come to see his delightful face for the last time because luckily, he saw their *real faces* when he was alive. Ozil had no one to be called as his relative, except Rohit, but in spite of that, a huge number of people were present during his cremation. Everyone was praying for his soul to rest in peace. I was not willing to bid the last goodbye to my friend. Instead I drove my two-wheeler to Ozil's house. The watchman opened the gate with tears in his eyes. "Who will I now wait for, madamji?" he asked, tears streaming down his face. I was too preoccupied with musing over the reason behind Ozil's suicide and didn't reply to him.

I entered the house from the main door and took my first step. The sound of each step was echoing in the house. Each and every corner of house was filled with a strange silence. Once his laughter had filled every empty space of the house with liveliness, but after his death, each and everything in his house became lacklustre. It seemed as if those insentient things were also in love with their owner. I was noticing everything, and at last the portrait of his wife 'Charulika' enmeshed my eyes. It was the same portrait I had seen a few years ago, but I felt like the smile which she had on her face had become wider that day. Her wait was now over! "Ozil reached the place where she had been waiting for him" I thought.

When I was observing everything acutely, I saw a white paper lying on a table in the living room. I was walking towards it slowly, but all of a sudden, a thunderstorm roared. That sound frightened me and I scurried off from the house. The watchman was standing outside waiting for me. I commanded him to lock the doors and headed towards my vehicle. I always strived hard to start its engine during rainy days. In the beginning, I tried to start it with self-start and then with kicks. I became so busy trying to launch my super vehicle that I skipped to notice the car that crossed the main gate of Ozil's house. Quickly I tried to look at the man who was driving the car but failed to do so. I thought of going back towards the house but unfortunately, as well as, fortunately my vehicle's engine was ready to ride. I turned back again and tried to identify the man, but all I got to see was a hazy figure. My brain's thought process mode got turned on. 'Ozil's near and dear ones were all present at his cremation. Then, who is this man who has come to his house? And why?' I wondered. I was driving and thinking, thinking and driving under a tempestuous sky. The drops of rainwater were soothing my over-wrought brain. Those cool and soft drops were alleviating my stress and compelling me to think that everything is destined, everything is pre-planned; even that suicide.

At midnight I was switching the lamp on and off, thinking continuously about the reason behind Ozil's self-slaughter. My heart was unable to digest that it was a suicide. When I was wondering about all this, his voice surrounded me saying - "Don't over think about anything; be hard-headed. Everything happens for a reason. Ruhani, promise me." I recalled the promise I had given to him.

 More than a week passed after Ozil's death but the police were still confused whether it was a case of suicide or murder. Observing my overthinking, my father found it better to share some words with me. He spoke -"Ruhani dear, I know the matter of Ozil's suicide is eating you from inside. AllI want to say is - don't do this. Do you have capacity to bring your friend back, baby? This overthinking is a slow poison. Don't repeat the mistake you committed few years back. We all love you. Groom yourself for a better future. It is not the end; it is the beginning of a new journey. Are you getting it?" He had serene face with hopes in his eyes. I was quiet. But then when my father left the room, I smiled and played the song which Ozil had recommended me to hear whenever I felt down.

"Zindagi ek safar hai suhana.

yahan kal kya ho kisne jaana."

The next morning, a thunderbolt was waiting for me. I saw my parents busy packing some stuff. They were surrounded by bags lying on the floor. I stepped out from the bed and walked there to find out what the matter was. I noticed that the stuff they were loading, were my belongings! "What's going on?" I asked. My father looked at me and said - "You forgot! The new session is starting after two days. You should reach there by tomorrow." The news was not at all invigorating. I wanted to unwind myself after bearing the shock of losing a dear friend, but everything happened in such a rapid way that it didn't give me a chance to mourn over the tragedy.

The day came when finally, for the first time I was going to live a life full of responsibilities, totally depending upon myself, all alone in a strange city surrounded by strange people. My father was determined to send me alone to a new city. He wanted to foster confidence in me.

Taking the luggage, we all reached the railway station. The weather was cold, the soft blowing air was caressing my face. Everyone was busy reaching the platform. We were walking carefully as some people were sleeping on the platform. I read my ticket - B2, Coach 37. Timing 5:50 A.M. Jodhpur to Jaipur. We entered in from the main gate. I counted my bags for the last time.

"Keep everything proper there, be careful of everything, and don't forget to take your medicines, and also be...." advised my mother but she was interrupted by my father - "Now will you please stop this?! Dear, study well there and never forget the norms of our family. I know you are my obedient child; you will never break our trust."

"I know papa." With tears in my eyes, I was pondering about the time spent with Ranil, which made me feel like a back-stabber. For my father, his family, his society, his kin overrode everything. Choosing my life partner by myself was surely a betrayal. He loves his daughter, but can keep her on stake when it comes to prestige of his family. Though his family had few of the men behind bars, but they never broke the law of their families and clan, so they were definitely the respected one.

The near-reaching Ranthambore Express broke the chain of my thoughts. I saw the train coming near me decelerating, concomitantly speeding my heartbeats. Though Jaipur was not an alien place for me, but for as long as anyone can remember, I was living in a cocoon. For every tiny work, I relied on my parents, but that day was the first step towards my journey of being independent. This drastic change in my life made my blood run cold. Nevertheless, deep inside I knew it is for my betterment.

I reminisced about the time spent with my family during my difficult days. The struggle was real, it was a Ruhani v/s Ruhani situation. Again, I had stumbled into a same situation. A positive Ruhani was standing on the platform with ambivalent thoughts. That chaos was so difficult to manage. In the fear of pushing myself into depression again by over-thinking, I quickly took a deep breath and I realized my potential. "You are stronger than you think. Don't do this to yourself. It is forbidden to harm mankind, then how can you do it to yourself? Self-harm is the heinous crime too. Stop doubting, start believing." Mumbling to myself, I looked at the firmament. In a fraction of second, I felt an ethereal sensation tingling my spine.

"Ruhani, give me this bag." Abruptly taking my bag off from my shoulder my mother smiled at me. "Hurry up my child, where are you lost? Why are you staring like this?" She spoke in a worried tone. Little did she know I was busy adoring how beautiful a woman could be.

A hustle started as soon as the train stopped but the one with reservations were at ease. Picking up my luggage my father headed ahead to find B2 coach. My mother and I soundlessly followed him with all the heavy stuff on my sensitive shoulders.

"Here it is, come fast, let's move in." With a slight smile on his face, my father stepped inside the train. Keeping the bags aside, he asked me to hand over the luggage I had. Following his words, I entered the train. Reaching the reserved seat number my parents properly arranged the bags near it. Near to my seat was sitting an old greybeard, busy reading a newspaper. Abruptly my father looked at him and said - "Hello sir, will you please take care of my daughter? She is travelling alone. Please let her know as soon as the train arrives at Jaipur Junction."

"Oh, surely sir" replied the man. Then, removing his spectacles he looked at me with slightly squeezed eyes and asked. "So, what are you studying beta?"

"Uncle, M.A in Political Science" I answered with slight hesitation. Being a sceptical sort, I rushed on to arranging the bags which were already arranged, just ignore more of his questions. The man was gentle enough to not to make me feel uncomfortable and turned his attention back to his newspaper.

Sitting near me, my parents were prompting me to face new challenges with valour and keeping my focus intact. Assuring them of conquering mountains, I embraced my mother. Suddenly, the train whistled, making whole family overwhelmed with emotions. The separation from my family was extremely excruciating. My father kissed me on my forehead and mother rained kisses on my cheeks. It was time to say the final goodbye. Leaving me alone in the train was a tough task for both them. My parents stood up slowly. Moving towards the exit both were successively looking back and waving at me till they alighted the train. My eyes became watery as they walked away from me. With a heavy heart, I waved back and I mumbled again to myself -"You are strong."

I made up my mind and the train made its engine ready to go ahead. I peeped out from the window to see everyone who came to bid me farewell. My father came near to the window and spoke - "Never get emotional thinking about us. We are always with you... we love you." Listening to his words, I started whimpering. I saw a strange remorse in his eyes which I never evinced in past. He looked at me as if I will never return and he has many things to speak to me, but was unable, or perhaps obliged.

The wheels of the train rolled. I wanted it to stop for moment just to talk to my father. 'What was he thinking? Which unspoken words were making him look restless?' As the train moved forward, my uneasiness heightened itself. I took a deep sigh and saw my close ones going blur as the vehicle distanced it from them. I wiped my tears. Stretching my back, I made myself comfortable on the seat.

"So, you are experiencing this for the first time, isn't it?" asked the old man who was allotted responsibility to be my train journey guardian by my parents.

"Yes Uncle."

"Oh, every child faces this emotional turbulence. My daughter too faced it, but today she is a doctor; so, it's going to give you lucrative consequences. Don't worry."

"Yes Uncle, definitely." With a smile on my face, I looked out from the window but my eyes were not in the mood to cherish the scenes outside. So, they decided to take nap. I fell asleep, accompanied by different dreams in the whole journey. Even my dreams were not mine, they all belonged to Ranil who was gazing at me but was not uttering a single word! What a pity! In my dreams too he does not speak anything to me. I was about to say something to him, but suddenly someone shook me and said, "Hey wake up, we are in Jaipur. You were in such a deep sleep. You must take care of it when you are travelling" said the gentle old man as he quietly picked up my bags.

"Uncle, please I can carry them…" Taking his age into concern I urged him many a times.

"Are you Hercules? You can't lift them all alone. Let me drop you to the taxi, let's go."

Pulling my luggage out from under the seat, I used all my strength to weigh it. I tried hard to sidestep everyone to alight the train and managed it somehow. The platform was crowded, which was an obvious thing, as it was the capital of the state. We both marched towards the exit. Making way through the throng with my bulky bags, we reached outside, where suddenly a few taxi drivers encircled us. "Ma'am, ma'am taxi service here, ma'am come here." Uncle ignored everyone, and made me sit in a taxi, which was spacious enough to carry my luggage. He didn't ask about the fare or anything else. Maybe he was in hurry. "Take care dear. Bye" Speaking these few words he went off to board a cab himself. He was walking fast with his bag resting on his shoulder. I was astounded and was hoping to meet same kind of people in this new city.

"Where do you want to go, ma'am?" the driver asked. I looked at the driver with suspicion. It was the first time that I was alone in a new city. Anyhow, I swallowed my fears and spoke - "Lal Kothi, near Apex Mall, B.R Oberoi college." Though I had visited the college for admission formalities with my father but that time I was uninvolved in observing the money he was spending at each step, including the fare. Thus, I didn't ask about the fare, as I had no idea about anything in that new city.

The slow speed of the taxi gave me a chance to observe my surroundings. The area outside Jaipur Junction was full of hustle bustle. A traffic police was striving to manage the traffic, but each individual there was trying to grab the opportunity to get out from the commotion across the road at the soonest. Slithering like a snake the taxi driver rolled the tyres of his taxi in a zig-zag pattern. Using all his tricks of passing from narrow ways he got out of the busy traffic zone. As he drove further, I found the city beautifully decorated with unique art at every spot. Most alluring was the Statue of Mahatma Gandhi and other freedom fighters depicting the Dandi March. Taking out my mobile phone, I cautiously started clicking pictures, saving them from getting blurred. At the same time, I saw the driver looking at me from the rear-view mirror confoundedly changing his facial expression. I even loved the clean wide roads and manageable traffic. I was relaxed to see the taxi seat having a 'Mahila Helpline number' written on it. At last, the driver stopped the taxi and announced "Ma'am here is your destination."

I stepped out with my baggage and searched inside my tote bag for my wallet. Mission accomplished, I paid the driver for his services and started walking towards my final destination - my college for post-graduation. Looking around, my eyes abruptly got fastened on a huge white shaded board, which read, 'B.R Oberoi College'.

I was standing on the gate of the college with mixed feelings of terror and jollity. My dim view forced me to doubt my capabilities, but a mirthful thought vanquished it in seconds. The white huge building was in front of me, with large posters hanging on its walls, "What are they all about? Elections may be." I mused. My eyes reached to the ground level where I saw some hostellers with their bags. I entered in and marched towards the office where the 'Trin Trin' sound was like a signature sound for that particular place. I joined the line and lingered for my turn. After a long wait I got a chance to peep inside the office from a small window.

"Hello sir, I am Ruhani Khan."

"Hmm... let me check." the person-in-charge said. He checked the list and said – "Room no.312".

"Ok sir, thank you." I replied, and left that place in search of my room. I clambered up the stairs with the heavy luggage on my back and in my hands. My awkward walk made everyone stare at me. Eventually walking through the corridors, I saw a board which read 312. I tried to open the door but it was locked from inside. I knocked twice and suddenly heard the voice – "Coming." A beautiful girl opened the door. She had dusky skin, good stature, round face, big shiny light brown eyes and cute small lips.

"Hey, hi." She greeted smiling broadly. "I am Ruby."

"Hi, I am Ruhani." Panting like a 100-metre race runner, I kept down my burdensome bags and smiled at her.

"Okay...so, are you my new roommate?" She asked looking at my bags like a custom officer. I smiled and nodded my head.

"I think you came early...?" I said, keeping my bags down on the floor.

"I came here yesterday. Truth is I can't live without this place; I really don't like staying at my home. I am living here from last three years. I had completed my U.G course in this college itself. Oh, you are still standing at the door, come in." Finally noticing me, she made a way.

I lifted my bags and entered inside. It was small room with two beds lying beside each other. The cupboards were in front of the beds and on the right side was a small window. There was a door beside the window which opened to washroom. The room was good and so was my bed. I jumped on the bed without bothering about unpacking my stuff. I was lying on my bed, trying to have a siesta for few hours.

"Hey Ruhani, don't you want to keep your stuff in your cupboard?"

"Actually… Ruby, I want to, but I am feeling tired" I said being annoyed by her suggestion.

"Oh… no problem, come I can help you."

I was worn out and wanted to bang Ruby's face on the wall, but I smiled, got up from the bed and started unpacking my bags.

Ruby was a friendly girl. She helped me in all matters related to the college, making it easier for me to sustain in the hostel environment.

Chapter 6
Initiating something new

The first day of the session came along with full of vim & vigour. That day I woke up much early. I was craving to attend my first lecture. Opening my 'Political Theory' book I randomly started reading the topics, so as to be quick in answering if the lecturer threw any question. Giving a knowledgeable dose to my brain, I later packed my college bag. It was 6:00 A.M when I opened my cupboard to choose the best dress to wear. A modish wine-shaded chiffon maxi top along with ice blue ankle jeans were best for the first day. Finishing a nice shower, I darted out from the washroom. After getting dressed, I tried to wake Ruby, but found her nonchalant in attending her first lecture. She prioritised her sleep over studies. After calling out to Ruby four to five times, I left her with her snooze and started walking towards the mess, which was to the left of our room. It was a big hall with gloomy walls and random coloured benches. Its kitchen slab was originally of white marble, which with time had transformed itself into yellowish brown. Entering inside, I saw the mess in-charge holding a big spoon. She knew I was clueless about 'what to do next'. "Pick up the plate. There. It is lying in that basket" she said slipping her hand inside her salwar's pocket. Taking her iPhone 3 out of it she looked at me. Ignoring her act, I picked up a plate and walked towards her. Serving two spoons of hot poha, she sat on a chair kept beside a huge utensil filled with poha.

The breakfast served to me had vegetables in it for namesake. Eating it, I counted two slices of tomato and six of onion. Only chillies were in abundant amount, which I hated the most. Chewing my food, I thought about my mother who always insisted me to eat paranthas as breakfast for my good health. That day I was recalling taste of her food and how much I was missing it, and her obviously.

Finishing my breakfast, I rushed out for attending the class. My hostel building was in the campus itself; it was almost 500 metres away from the college building. First day of the college looked exhilarating, most of the students were busy in finding their classrooms, while other group of students were sitting on the stairs holding registers in their hand. I geared myself to find my lecture hall.

"Hello ma'am can you please tell me where MA part 1 political science lecture hall is?" I asked a random girl passing by.

"I am sorry, I don't know, but the notice-board can help you."

"Oh …Thank you" I felt so dumb at that moment! I instantly regretted asking her and headed towards the notice-board. On the board, the way to the various lecture halls were written in tandem with some notices. The information pinned on it helped me showing the way. Obeying what the board instructed me, I crossed a 10-foot-wide corridor with cream-coloured tiles on the floor, freshly painted white walls, and wooden slates which announced the name and number of the lecture halls. Finally, I encountered a wooden slate which read - 'MA Political Science Part 1 Lecture Hall'. I entered the hall and grabbed the middle bench. The hall was spacious with large white board. There was a small stage-like structure on which a small iron table was kept with a microphone and markers on it. While I was busy noticing the lecture hall keenly, I heard a voice coming from my left side.

"Hey hi, are you new here?" A boy asked sitting beside me. The person was not less than a main lead from super hero movies. He was tall, with a wheatish complexion and a knock-out personality.

"Yes I am."

"Ok, so what's your name?"

"Ruhani" I said. "And yours?"

"Rushil." He replied. The boy was charming, his curiosity matched that of a child's. He was eager to know everything about me.

"Good morning sir." All the students present in the lecture hall wished the lecturer when he entered in.

"Good morning class." he wished back and then added, "So today is our first lecture. Should I teach you or should I tell you something really important in relation to our lives?"

Everyone preferred the second option, so did I and Rushil, but our intention to prefer the second option was not to actually know about our lives. Instead, we wanted to continue with our chat. Like a child, he kept on asking questions to me. Questions about my family, where I came from, and so on

I was answering those questions which I felt to be answered.

"So how many members you have in your family?" I asked him.

"Ohh... mumma... papa and my elder brother. We four, or you could say, they three." His face was darkened saying this.

"Why so?" I asked with concern.

"Well, from class 11th I am here in Jaipur. I was forcibly sent here by my parents. I never had a convivial relationship with my elder brother. Comparison between both of us by my parents and relatives shattered our relation. To the extent that, my brother too started looking at me as inferior. I hardly visit my family now. This college is my home. I love this place; I feel peaceful and serene here."

"And we are your family" I said and smiled at him. He smiled listening to my words. I felt sad for him; in spite of lack of love from his family's side, he was twinkling. Of course, that smile wasn't a real one. It was a blend of 'desire of love from family' and 'what can I do about it, I have to live like this'. But why was he telling me everything?

"Umm, I hope you are not finding it uncomfortable that I am sharing all this with you after having met just a few minutes ago? I am also not understanding why I feel drawn to tell you everything. Are you finding it awkward?" Rushil asked, himself finding it sticky to reveal about his relation with family. Truth was, it was very rare for him to get to speak to someone who wouldn't judge him.

"There is no problem. Don't worry, I am not judging you, or your family. You can revivify your relation with them, understand them, and try to make them understand you. You can't be a photocopy of your brother. Make them realise that they are busy their own loving expectations from their son, but not their son." I whispered without blinking my eyes, talking to him, like there was a child in front of me.

Gazing at me, Rushil whispered- "Looking at you I got a hint that your talks do possess depth in them. You are not a girl who just witters all the time."

"Ok class, so end of the discussion, we will meet tomorrow" suddenly the lecturer's voice boomed. But finding a person taking a shine to my advice sparked interest in me to carry on with the conversation, as our discussion was still remaining. I wanted to chat more with him.

"So.... do you want to have coffee?" he asked – his face displaying nervousness laced with the hope of a positive response from me.

"Aah... Yes, why not?" I replied ditheringly, as I never opened up much with someone I just met an hour ago. 'Okay Ruhani, now don't act too much reserved, you already had a long conversation with him' I mumbled to myself.

As we were walking downstairs to the canteen, most of the girls had their eyes on Rushil. Some were smiling at him; some were approaching him just to say Hi.

Like a bus stopping at every stop, I and Rushil were applying brakes at every girl who approached him. They talked to him, flirted with him and his response encouraged them even more but most of the time he seemed vexed and showed some of them impudence.

"Rushil, I am starving, can I proceed to the canteen please?"

"Oh... I am sorry, let's go." He answered understanding my situation. "I am sorry for all this, actually it's all the fault of my popularity." Winking at me, he tried to show off his fame in that college.

"Yes, and of your personality too." I spoke making a poker face, revealing my least interest in his popularity.

He beamed and continued to talk. We both reached the canteen. I found it the most thrilling place of the college. It seemed like every student was having ceaseless merriment there. The round red tables surrounded by circles of friends was actually showing how exotic college life is. Rushil and I found a table away from the crowd.

"So Ruhani, do you have a photo of your parents?"

"Yeah, I do have pictures of them in my phone; but why? What happened?"

"I just assumed looking at you that your parents must be a beautiful couple."

"Hahaha, actually I am a magician who conquered this beauty with my magic" I gave him an insane answer. For that I still feel regretful; why had I acted like this? Had all sensible replies run out from my head at that time? Whatever, but he turned to be a PhD holder in flirting.

"Oh, so you are magician! Okay. Now I realised why I am feeling so lost as if someone hypnotized me. Was it due to your magic?"

"Haven't you confronted magicians before?"

"I have, but never met someone like you." Folding his hands, he leaned on his chair's back.

"What?" I said. 'What am I supposed to speak now? He is flirting with me. None of the boys I knew till date had flirted with me like this. I mean, what kind of flirting is this? This can be called as innocent flirting, done by those who actually don't know what to do, but still try their best." I thought. I was having fun. He made me laugh with his good-natured banter.

After spending a good time with him it was time for me to leave for hostel. Walking slowly in bright sunlight, I was relishing the view of the neem trees, sparrows, and squirrels all through the way. I was finding them full of life. It made me glance inside me. Yes, I had a mask of happiness on my face, but it was just that – a mask. Truth was, I had never recovered wholly. I discovered this when Ozil left my life. I was still mourning for that loss from within. Reaching my room, I changed my clothes and comfortably laid on my bed. Though I had come to a new city with much positivity in me but it was so short termed. I observed my behavioural pattern. I was relying more on other people for my happiness. Why was I unable to feel happiness within me?!"

Still finding Ruhani in the same position, the nurse Anjali shared her thoughts once more "When we are channelling our happiness through external sources then how can we ever find that solace and serendipity forever? You got scholarship - you became happy. You came to new city - you became happy. You got a job - You became happy. Notice how every smile on your face comes with a condition, and all conditions are connected with external sources. Are you understanding, it's like- 'If I get this, will I be happy'?"

"You are right, my every happiness was connected with some condition, which was temporary."

"I can understand. First Ranil, who you saw as your saviour, and then Ozil, your true friend who was actually your saviour - both the losses were big deal in their own way, but the baggage of your past was much bigger than that."

"Hmm... but I was still alive on that battlefield. I knew I needed to live this life anyhow. I re-focussed on my studies and college and was ready for the next day. Entering my lecture hall, I saw Rushil standing with a new boy. I didn't know who he was."

"Hi Ruhani." Saying this he waved at me. Since our first day together had been so cordial, I preferred to not take a turn and walk straight towards him.

"Hi Rushil." I greeted at while looking at the boy standing beside.

"Meet him; he is my friend Ansh." Introducing me to Ansh, Rushil hit Ansh's giant stomach with his elbows. Oh, that cute, not-so-fit boy was trying best to hide his pain. I laughed and sat on the first bench. They both sat on the bench just next to mine.

Attending all the classes we three proceeded towards the canteen where I saw Ansh's tummy accepting all kinds of food which made him an obesity-stricken person. He was a reflection of Rushil but lacked the quality of being flirty, though in awkward way. The melange of us three resulted in a hilarious trio.

With flowing time, Ansh became my good friend too, but it was Rushil with whom I spent most of my time. Initially he seemed to me a supercilious person but he had a vibrant personality for which I craved for. His positivity was changing me internally. He was witty, self-possessed, and most importantly, a fashionable man of. He even became my personal stylist. With his advice, for the first time ever, I went for hair re-bonding and highlights, and I didn't regret it. That hair makeover, without doubt, made me look breathtakingly beautiful. Rushil would also accompany me whenever I was out for shopping. He had an impressive choice in all spheres, especially in matter of clothes. His every pick had quality of being natty. He knew which clothes and dresses would suit me more than I did.

Once he gifted me a pair of fancy red pencil heels. I was worried just looking at the height of those heels! "How will I walk wearing these high heels, Rushil?!"

"Oh, common Ruhani, you can."

"Hmm... okay, I will wear them when a deserving person arrives in my life who will save me from stumbling."

"Oh, till then I will save you." Speaking innocently his eyes bore into mine. For few seconds I was bewitched by his deep brown eyes, which were gazing at me without blinking.

"Hehe, you always shield me Rushil. I don't need these heels to make you save me, hehehehe" I cackled, just for sake of unlocking our eyes and fleeing from that awkward moment. Though the quality of healthy flirting was inculcated in his personality, but somewhere I knew he wasn't just flirting aimlessly at that moment.

I realized my importance in his life when once I went to a mall, which was located at the back of beyond. Carrying shopping bags, strolling on the path outside the mall I noticed few young men following me. Spooked, I sped up my steps and they did the same. With feelings of trepidation, I rang up the only person who popped into my mind - Rushil. He too was terrorized when I informed him about my situation. Advising me to walk into a crowded place, he told me not to disconnect the call and continue talking until he arrived. Little did he know that the place was a prime example of 'isolated one'.

Crossing my fingers, I was desperately waiting for him. Despondency coated my every inch, my mind pushed me towards the consequences, thinking if those men grappled me, then which techniques should I use to attack back? Walking ahead was seeming an unsafe option to me, so I stopped near a signboard making myself ready for action. I also prepared myself by typing the Mahila Helpline no. on my keypad. Later, I turned my head to see that group, and saw the men coming near me. My heart started pounding furiously.

Each step taken by those men felt like a vile menace approaching me. Watching their movements carefully, I braced myself to face the tragedy with valour. 3 2 1, I was all set. Everything was ready.

Thanks to heaven, they all walked forward and sat in a car parked under the tree. God! I took a sigh of relief and chided myself for my dumb act. I had even shaken up Rushil with my frightened words, for no reason. That incident made me dive into the feeling of a woman who actually faces such kind of tragedies. Standing alone, I cursed myself for misjudging the men, though I was still terrified thinking about what if the situation got reversed.

After a few minutes, I saw Rushil's car swiftly coming towards me. Applying brakes, he leapt out from the car. I, with a 'sorry face' sprinted towards him. He embraced me with care. Asking me about the men he tenderly stroked my face and berated me for not being heedful.

"Actually Rushil, they weren't a threat for me. I just misjudged them" I confessed lowering my gaze. I was sorry for making him tensed. Rather than going ballistic, he beamed at me and we left the place.

"Your friend Rushil, actually sounds like a Superman. Such a wonderful person he seems. Did you never feel like he is the one for you?" asked an enraptured Anjali.

Oh... never, he was my friend. Yes, he was handsome, humorous, caring, but it wasn't he who was a problem; it was me. I was still obsessed with Ranil. I eagerly wanted him to come back in my life. I wanted to know the reason he had left me without saying a word. We shared beautiful memories, and I was unable to forget them.

"Oh?! Not even after Rushil gifted you such a treasure of memories which you are still recalling with twinkling eyes?" sarcastically and softly spoke the nurse who got to know the things which were still hidden for Ruhani.

"Rushil and my case was totally different, we were friends."

"Have you never felt as if you were controlling your feelings so as to not to get hurt once more, because this time you were cautious that you both don't hold future together?" Trying to explain Ruhani with a smile on her face, Anjali pushed her into thinking deeply.

No, no... I know the reason more than you do. I knew Ranil would arrive anytime soon. Was it possible to confront him after being in someone's else arms? My love for him was true and pure. I didn't want to stand in front of him with regrets. I wanted him to know that I always waited for him."

"Hmmm, Ruhani, don't take me wrong. It's a simple advice as a friend. Don't feel guilty when you are actually not. There exist people called narcissists, who are there to make you feel like a culprit, manipulate you, and snatch your real identity from yourselves." Anjali had got a hint from Ruhani's words that the woman is suffering from low self-esteem and co-dependency. Seeing Ruhani losing herself in the depth of her words, she quickly added - "So you had lovely friendship with Rushil.... then?"

"Yeah.... indeed. We spent our time studying in library for hours, we chatted almost about everything. We would never face a dearth of topics to have a conversation. Strolling in the corridor became our habit. Many lectures were attended and many were bunked. Many discussions took place and many arguments flared up, and between all of these things, our friendship blossomed like it would never wither. With passing time, I explored Rushil thoroughly. I became fan of his healthy flirting. He teased me a lot and always made me laugh, but he never spoke anything which could have rubbed me the wrong way. He knew his limits. Sometimes I found his talks odd. There were many instances when he seemed so inclined towards unearthly issues. He loved to travel in a transcendent world of fantasies. I found that thing strange, but apart from that, every trait of his was astounding."

"Oh... did he ever give you any hint during those days that he feels differently for you?" Anjali asked with curiosity, wanting to know more about this person.

"Well, every day through his gestures I somewhere knew he has feelings for me, but I was unsure, because hitherto he hadn't uttered a single word about it. I remember, on one pleasing twilight, I was ambling in the park with him. I was walking with a broad smile and chuckle. I don't know why I was so happy that day, but sometimes you do feel happy without reason.

Walking with me on that path, Rushil did try to convey me something.

"Ruhani..." he ventured.

"Yes?"

"What kind of person do you want to marry?" He asked looking straight into my eyes.

"Well, I don't want to marry anyone, but if a person is compatible with me, then I will definitely consider him."

"That's what I am asking. What qualities do you want in your partner to match the compatibility level?"

"Hmmm, firstly basic things, like honesty, no lies, understanding nature etc. On the next level, I want him to be my best friend. He should be a grounded person. We must not have any insecurities in our relationship. Mutual trust should be limitless. We should welcome each other's weirdness without putting it in basket of embarrassment, and stand up for each other crossing all the odds. Ups & downs in relationship are inevitable, but we both should keep aside our egos and be open for any kind of conversation. Isn't it an ideal bond, huh...?" Taking a deep sigh with smiling face I got carried away while speaking about the relation I always desired for, like I always do.

"That would be a beautiful relation! How easy and smooth life would become when we have such kind of a partner and relation" Rushil commented with a cute smile. The intensity in his eyes was pulling me towards it. His eyes were similar with Ranil's, so deep, so expressive. But I quickly looked to the other side and said,

"Yes, but why are you asking me these questions? Never heard such kind of serious words from you!"

"Oh, come on, nothing serious" he said, thumping me on the back, trying to make me comfortable and distract me from what I was thinking.

After some time, he asked me in a soft voice,

"Ruhani? Were you in love with someone?"

As yet I was ambling, feeling like a feather. But his question paused my steps. I stared at him with a blank face. Though many of our friends ask about exes, but the way he asked stood out from the rest.

"Are your dewy eyes the answer to my question?" As soon as Rushil spoke this, I was reduced to tears. Watching my heart sink, he embraced me tenderly. I too chained my hands around his back.

When he was comforting me, I suddenly became aware of what I was doing. Getting out of his arms I apologised, since I found it wrong. Then, deliberately ignoring him, I reversed my steps and started walking away as fast as I could. I kept giving myself all the curses and abuses I knew!

Rushil and I never had any further discussion about that moment. We acted as if something like that had never happened. Nevertheless, the awkwardness of that incident lived in my mind for a long time.

*

Chai-Chaska, the only munching station with reasonable rates for me and Ansh. It was a small cafe with four coffee tables each having two floral designed wing chairs arranged parallel to each other. Embellished with golden metal pendant lamps hung above the tables with their lights focusing on its centre, the cafe was overall easy on the eye.

It was fun thing for me and Ansh that the cafe had no other guests except us - the bunkers. Keeping his bag on the table, he sat and bounced on a padded chair "Wow, so comfortable! Why can't the iron chairs of our classes be replaced with these? Those hard chairs give me so much pain."

"Leave the chairs. We are alone here. We can talk loudly Ansh. This is the actual comfort for me."

Rushil hardly joined us in cafes and restaurants. The health and gym freak guy never understood our love for food.

Having light conversation, guffawing and giving high-fives on every senseless chatter, we found our energy draining out. Ordering crispy garlic bread and butter Maggi, we set ourselves back to chat mode.

After few minutes opening a different topic Ansh spoke taking a big bite of garlic bread. "Ruhani, when are you planning to get married?"

"Not so soon Ansh. I need to build my career first."

"Yeah, that's right, so it's going to be a love marriage or arrange marriage?"

Though I was engaged, I didn't want to disclose my secret to Ansh but I spoke my heart out saying, "Actually Ansh I don't think I am made to play a puppet by having an arrange marriage. I don't believe in arranged marriages. I mean, how can you be with a person without having the 'This is the one' factor when you look at him? I don't mean it's a bad thing, but I don't think it'll ever work out for me."

"Okay; and what about love marriage? Hasn't that 'This is the one' kind of a person arrived in your life yet?"

His words paused me and I was struck with enigma for a moment. Unknowingly, I lowered my gaze. Once again, Ranil invaded the place I had kept reserved for him in my thoughts. Somehow, I answered, "Well I haven't found that special person yet, but hopes are always alive."

"What happened? You are sounding low."

"Ahmmm, nothing."

"Ruhani, have you never experienced love?"

"Ahmm...never." Blinking my eyes incessantly, I found myself in a strained condition.

"Maybe that person you are searching for, is near you."

The man was already breaking my spine, and if he added even one more sentence, he would surely make my blood boil. I scowled at Ansh willing him to button his lips.

"No, no, I am not talking about me, don't take me wrong" he stammered, trying to handle the fire in me.

I knew to whom he wanted to mention. Shaking my head, I smiled at him- "I know it Ansh. I can see that person's inclination towards me; but you know, love is a special feeling. You can't feel it for every boy who is good to you. Rushil is a very dear friend of mine. I don't want to mar our friendship by giving it a tag of a relationship."

"Ruhani, don't do this. I know he is flirty, maybe he is not up to the mark according to you, but he is the one for you. Believe me."

"No Ansh, you don't know anything about me. I can't love anyone; I don't want to love anyone. I adore Rushil extremely, but loving someone is so difficult."

"Ruhani, it's not. To love is not a task to measure on the level of difficulty. Just think about it - how perfect you both are for each other!"

"Ansh, you know my answer."

"This is the problem with every girl nowadays. When a boy loves a girl from the core of his heart, she hurls him into the 'friend zone'. You are committing the same mistake Ruhani" he shouted at me ill-manneredly. I had never seen Ansh behaving like this.

"Ansh...will you please change the topic? You are pissing me off." I was trying to resist him for the sake of avoiding this discussion about love. To love someone again with the same depth was impossible for me. I always had a fear of remaining empty-handed at last. It had happened with me in the past. It happens many a times that you love someone, spend beautiful moments together, become a power couple, and in the end, leave each other to spend your life with an unknown person. The last bit especially happens in India a lot, because arranged marriages are still a norm here. Leaving each other for families and society is common. However, some people are born with diamond in their hearts, their love is remains solid. In spite of all the odds, they end up being together, but they are rare, very rare.

My words submerged Ansh into agitation. He started throwing audacious remarks at me. "Ruhani, I never knew that even you belong to the category of those girls who use boys for beer and skittles. You watch movies with them in multiplexes, hit the streets, you need grand cuisine in opulent restaurants and when they confess their feelings, you all change and act like a bitch."

"Ansh...this is vicious! Don't you think you are going too far?! I know there must be girls like that, but tagging all the girls like that is wrong. I never used Rushil. I am self-dependent. Ask Rushil how many times he paid for my bills, and how much I contributed whenever we went for an outing. Just because you are reluctant to pay for yourself, throwing all your expenses on Rushil, doesn't mean each of his friends is doing the same! One more thing: some of you have a special kind of problem with girls. If we don't friend-zone a boy who wants to be with us, and keep welcoming him, then you will call us promiscuous woman, whore or whatever. But if we give a clear indication of our feelings, then too it's our mistake. If Rushil is not forcing me, then why are you creating problems? And yeah... here is my contribution." Speaking in one breath I took out 300 rupees from my wallet and kept them on the table. I started crying, I never expected Ansh to be like this. Ansh stood in silence. After a minute he came closer and tried to wipe my tears apologising to me at the same time. My anger was at its peak. I pushed Ansh away and went out of the cafe, making it our last conversation.

Ansh tried hard to normalise the things, but it went out of bounds as time. I knew Ansh didn't tell Rushil the reason behind the suddenly frosty relationship between us two. Although Rushil tried hard to bring the same bond between three of us, but it was beyond the bounds of possibility, because neither Ansh nor I wanted to revivify our dead friendship.

No doubt Rushil was up to the scratch, but I kept him on the level of a friend. Firstly, I was not clear about my feelings for him. Secondly, Ranil never left his place from my heart; and lastly, I didn't want to get myself indulged in those feelings which could have hurt me again.

Rushil and Ruby were my only friends now. I wanted both of them to meet each other. Ruby was doing her M.A in History, a different department. So, we never got a chance to be together. Also, she hardly attended her classes, thus making her trips to the college very rare.

One day I made a plan. I called Rushil to the canteen and took Ruby with me. Ruby and I were sitting inside. After a few minutes, I saw Rushil entering through the canteen door. I shouted with excitement -

"Hey Rushil, we are here."

Moving forward, Rushil noticed Ruby and raised his pie hole's cupid bow. Ruby also saw him. After staring at him for some time, she spread her chapped lips into a small smile. In contrast to her Rushil seemed a bit awkward. Putting his hands in his pockets, he tilted his neck, and looked at me with knitted brows. Dazed with what I was experiencing around me, I silently waited for both of them to tip their hats to each other. However, they neither welcomed each other, nor were they in good spirits to see each other.

I felt like it was miscalculated plan. Ruby's face was already pale with woe. Swiftly she took her steps towards exit and escaped from the scene. Rushil too was looking discomposed. He looked at me and said, "What a surprise? You wanted me to meet her? Seriously!"

"Yes, I wanted you to meet her. She is my roommate and without doubt my good friend. Why you can't befriend her, she is a nice girl?"

"You are still a child. Is it your age to force friendships on people? That's great if she is your good friend. Nice for you. But I choose my friends wisely, not by force." Rushil's words made me feel unendurable; he was never ungracious before.

"Mind your tongue Rushil. You are judging my intentions without a hitch. Why will I force you?

I just wanted to introduce you both." I was vexed and wanted to leave that place, but he stopped me grabbing my hand and replied- "Look Ruhani, I am sorry for whatever I spoke. I didn't mean that; you know me so well. But listen, this girl is a green-eyed queen. You are committing a grave mistake by not trying to know who she really is."

"Shut up Rushil, now you are judging her."

"Ruhani, I don't want to judge any girl. But what I am saying not about any gender; it's about only that particular person. If she is girl doesn't mean she can't be wrong. Look, she will definitely order you to stop talking to me. She was the girl who used to follow me everywhere from the first day of the college during our under-graduation days. She was infatuated with me. One day she proposed to me. Looking at her extreme dedication I said 'yes'. Later I realized the shallowness in her dedication. Nothing was special, just a tag of girlfriend and boyfriend was handling our relationship. I knew it was not going to last. I was simply a 'Ye mera hoke rahega' challenge for her. She succeeded in it, but I became a fool. Ansh once caught her kissing a boy from the science department. She cheated on me. I never looked at her again and walked out silently from her life. Consequently, the girl spread claptrap rumours about me in the entire college."

"Enough Rushil, stop it." I shouted and fled away jerking his hand. Walking towards my hostel the flashback of Rushil speaking those words were banging my mind incessantly. They were pinching me and piercing my ears like hot iron rods. I opened the door of my room and saw Ruby standing, facing the window. "I am sorry Ruby" I said. She turned around and promptly turned back without replying. It irked me.

"Listen Ruby, I am really sorry, it wasn't my intention to hurt you" lowering my gaze I apologised again.

"No Ruhani, you don't need to. You didn't know anything, it's ok." She talked to me in a soft tone, but didn't explain herself.

At night when we were lying on the bed, Ruby called out to me.

"Ruhani."

Coming out of my late-night musings, I turned towards her and whispered- "Yes."

"Listen Ruhani, you are a benign person and I can't see anything pernicious happening with you. I want you to maintain distance from Rushil. He is not what you are thinking. He can prove to be very deceitful. Bloody womanizer!" Ruby spoke in vexation, showing her concern for me. I was ambivalent about her intentions as she spoke the same words which Rushil told me that she will. Now I was confused. Was this indeed Ruby's reality??

"Listen Ruby, you might be thinking that something is cooking between me and him, but no, I don't have such feelings for him. My feelings are still trapped for a guy who I want to forget, but I can't. I am helpless, I want to come out of that mess" I yelled in distress as the horrifying flashbacks started coming back.

"Ruhani, listen dear, don't cry. Tell me the matter." Ruby came near and embraced me putting her warm hand on my shoulder.

I told her the whole story; my every word was accompanied by tears.

"Stop crying, Ruhani. You are a strong girl. If someone left you that's his mistake." Like every good friend says, she too told me that I deserve someone better.

"Ruhani, don't punish yourself, heartbreaks turn us into tormented souls, but that doesn't mean we should encircle ourself with our past memories only. You should move on and one more thing, I am always with you."

Ruby got sentimental, but it was infeasible for me to make her understand how hard I tried to dismantle the feelings. The person left me without speaking anything. I always ruminated about the reason he left me for. Many a times I decided to forget him, but every time it proved to be a bootless attempt.

"One more thing Ruhani, I hope you won't meet Rushil again." That was the last advice she gave me.

Dubiously looking at her I nodded my head agreeing in front of her, but how could I leave one of my good friends just for the sake of their personal hostility? Listening to her for an hour I went to my laptop and typed the 876th mail to Ranil. Yes, it was still my habit to tell him everything through mails. He never replied to any, but this fact never stopped me from sending him long messages. I always had hope that one day he will respond to them.

In spite of Ruby's negative statements about Rushil, I maintained good relations with him. However, I was reluctant to believe the words he spoke for Ruby.

*

18th September was Rushil's birthday. I bought him some gifts - a Zebronics Bluetooth headphone, a 'best friend' trophy from Archie's, a handmade scrap book which included our indelible moments together, and also planned a surprise party for him. Looking at all fancy things Ruby asked me for who they were. I found it better to not mention Rushil's name. I told her the gifts were for Riddhi, one of my classmates, but I was stupid to lie. I forgot, she was his ex, and she knew to who this day belongs. Still in contact with Rushil and telling a lie about the gifts were the two heinous crimes I had committed, according to her. After a while I evinced the real Ruby whom I never knew. I can't bring myself to speak the words she used for him. It was Rushil's birthday and I didn't want myself to engage in any kind of drama. Saying 'whatever' I quickly got out of that yolk, walking away from her.

 Crossing the main gate of the hostel I saw a desert-shaded Royal Enfield with a hunky man sitting on it. Coming close, I experienced relief being beside him.

"Happy Birthday Idiot." Giving him a side hug, I shouted in joy. "May your every wish come true and you get everything you wish for. God bless you Rushil." Resting my hand on his shoulder, I beamed gladly.

"And I hope God listens to this prayer of yours" he replied softly. Beneath his goggles, I saw his eyes continuously looking at me. Finding this a little weird I snapped my fingers to break his gaze.

"You are looking different today Ruhani. This sea-green salwar-suit is complementing your beauty" he again spoke in a soft tone.

"Hehe...seriously." Finding it weirder, I avoided further discussion on my looks and sat on the back-seat.

"Okay! So where are we going?"

"Umm...follow the directions I give."

"OK Ma'am."

Rushil carried a torch for solitary places. In spite of being an extrovert he needed his 'me time'. There is no surprise if you ever see him sitting alone in a cafe totally engrossed in reading books. So, I planned to celebrate his birthday at Sky Beach, a beautiful beach theme-based restaurant, tranquil and all white.

I was in contentment when I saw his glowing face; he loved ambience of the place. He walked near and enfolded me in his arms – "Thank you so much Ruhani for bringing me here, this place is beautiful." That moment made me proud of my decision. Releasing me from his embrace, he again glanced around admiringly to have a view of the restaurant. "I must say, this is a really beautiful place. It's a surprise I never heard of it before. Come, let's sit here." Praising the restaurant, he sat on the couch and patted the seat, signalling me to sit beside him. I smiled and sat with my legs crossed. With a slow sweet smile, he once more thanked me for making him feel special.

"Rushil, please don't over-react! Won't you do same for me? Hehe."

"Nope, never, these kinds of arrangements belong to someone special." With a straight face he mocked me, thinking it would lead me into jealousy. Haah, his mistake! I was so calm and okay. Oh, actually, to tell the truth, inside I was not. Ignoring his words, I reached into my bag. When it comes to giving surprises, I think I am the most impatient person. I quickly took out all the gifts, and kept them on the table.

"All for me!?" He was amazed, unable to believe it. He again asked me about those gifts.

"Yes, all for you! Now open them." I wanted him to unwrap the gifts without taking much time. I was eager to see his reaction. Opening the box of the headphone his first words were "Ruhani, there was no need to spend this much."

I was not in mood to answer Rushil, because I was able to see his overwhelming happiness. Like a child he started unwrapping the other gifts. Smiling continuously, he opened the other two gifts as well. He loved the headphones as he was crazy for music. He loved the 'best friend' trophy because he found it creative. But the gift he adored endlessly was the scrapbook, because it was about us; our friendship. While turning its every page, he had a sparkly smile on his face.

"Everything you have done for me was amazing Ruhani! Thank you so much! he said, turning another page of the scrapbook.

"Rushil, now shut it. You can watch it later. I have heard that this restaurant serves delish Mexican Dishes, let us order that."

few friends of Rushil's were waiting for him at another cafe. Since it was already late, I told him to go ahead to that cafe directly rather than dropping me first. He denied this idea initially, but my stubbornness finally made him say 'Take care and call me when you reach home' and he left the place.

Chapter 7
The Day which changed it all

Many of our classmates misunderstood me and Rushil as lovers, but we were not. Rushil was my admirer, so was I. The time we spent together over-rided all the moments I shared with other college friends. My heart was very much contended by his actions. There were many instances when I felt like I had fallen for him but I don't know what was impeding me from making a forward move. I was sandwiched between my mind and my heart. Each of my efforts to dedicate myself fully to Rushil, proved futile. First reason was, I myself wanted to be stuck for Ranil, I don't know why? Also, the idea of marrying a person belonging to different clan would have filled my family with abhorrence. That was the difference between what I felt for Ranil and for Rushil. In the case of Ranil the difference of religion never troubled me but in the case of Rushil, it did. I never imagined myself taking a stand for him where I would confront my family. Becoming ambivalent about my feelings for Rushil I dropped the idea of devoting myself to him and retained the same old relation of friendship.

The calendar was passing with supersonic speed. Two years of my post-graduation passed like a moment captured in a camera. In those two years I never a got chance to do the thing I loved most – reading stories and novels. Although the part 2 exams were approaching in few days, but I was valiant enough to read an out-of-syllabus book which could unwind me during those hectic hours.

To fulfil my desire, I went to our college library. It was a big hall with a variety of books. It looked like a silent valley where only the humming of fans was audible. From the stacks of books arranged there, I started searching for a book which could have matched my mood. The bookshelves were full of 'knowledge giving treasure'. I went from one book shelf to another. Suddenly my eyes saw a book titled catchily as, 'The Spirits'. The red coloured book looked fascinating. I took it and approached librarian to get it issued in my name. The librarian gave me a weird look after reading the title of the book. Wordlessly, he issued it to me and finally the book was under my possession. Keeping it in my bag I proceeded to my room, which I wanted change. I had written many applications to my hostel warden regarding this matter, but a vacant spot in another room wasn't in my destiny. The only option left with me was to live with Ruby and adjust.

Knocking the door, I casually looked around corridor.

"Hey, Nisha was looking for you, she was asking for your maroon heels, but I denied" said Ruby, tying her hair into a knot as she walked towards her bed.

"Hmm... Thank you. I hope she won't come again" I uttered lazily, latching the door. My relation with Ruby had dwindled after she gave me false information about Rushil, not once but every-time when we would talk anything related to boys or relationships. In spite of that, I never told her that Rushil and I still shared a healthy bond. I also did not want to become Rushil's advocate. I knew him well, so her talks which were aimed at besmirching his name, never mattered.

 Laying on the bed she looked at me - "Where were you?" she asked squinting her eyes.

"I went to the library today. Got myself an extremely interesting book."

"Oh really, then show me! What it's about?"

I started searching the book in my bag which contained almost everything, including that red book. I pulled it out and handed it over to Ruby. Reading the title – 'The Spirits' - Ruby's facial expressions changed! Her face turned pale and eyes grew wide out of shock. I was unable to sense the reason behind her unexpected reaction.

"Hey Ruby, what happened? Don't be such a coward! It's just a title" I said keeping my hand on her shoulder.

"It's not about cowardice, Ruhani. This book is responsible for turning an irreproachable person into a fallen angel. I don't want anyone now to move in that direction."

 "I don't think this book contains any kind of perilous stuff. Why would the librarian have kept it if it was so risky?"

"No, the book doesn't, but its title does affect the person reading the book. He becomes curious to get himself introduced to a different world."

"Oh! You seem to know someone who went through this, isn't it Ruby? Who was that person? Tell me?" I asked showing fake curiosity, mocking her for making such a stupid statement.

"No, I can't. Anyways am I obliged to answer all your queries? No! So now, go to sleep. I am feeling drowsy" she spoke churlishly and opened her pink fluffy blanket to hide herself in it.

I kept the book aside and lay down on the bed. Ruby's wretched behaviour made me cheerless. I was wondering how could this girl have tried everything to ruin someone's name? That time I wanted to vanquish the bulkiness of my heart by talking to someone who could have waned my sorrows. Suddenly my phone rang showing Rushil's number. I picked up the call and ran towards the balcony.

"Hello Ruhani."

"Hello Rushil." I spoke in an afflicted manner, slowly sitting in a corner of the balcony.

"What happened? You are not sounding good."

"Hmm, nothing I am fine. Tell me what happened? Something important?"

"No, first tell me what happened?" He asked again, and I denied, again.

"Hmmm, it's okay if you don't want to tell me. Actually, I have a plan for tomorrow. You know that our graduation is at its climax, so I thought that these remaining days should be spent with each other in an exciting way. What do you think about an outing tomorrow?"

"Yes, why not? I will definitely be there. Tell me the place."

"No, I will come to pick you up."

"Oh… fine, as you wish."

"Ok done then, tomorrow be ready at 7:00 A.M."

"Done, byeeeee, good night" I said, smiling like an idiot.

It was fun listening about the idea of spending tomorrow's day with Rushil's exuberant personality, but I was still thinking about Ruby's unusual behaviour. I knew she was wooden-headed but her words literally bewildered me. "What was the hint behind telling me all those things?" I wondered.

Pondering over the reasons, I fell asleep. The deep sleep made me remember something which was had been retained in the unquenchable side of my heart. I saw Ranil in my dream. He was coming towards me, looking into my eyes and standing in front of me. But then he started walking away without showing any concern for me. That small dream woke me up. I checked my mobile phone to see the time; it was 3 AM. Unable to sleep again, I stepped down from the bed and walked to the balcony. It was a dark, moonless night, but the scintillating stars were having a tranquilizing effect on my eyes. It was the month of February; the soft-blowing cold air of spring was fondling me. I was yearning for Ranil. I closed my eyes and spoke - "Hope a day comes when I find you standing beside me." I stood at that place for few minutes. Suddenly, I felt someone standing behind me. I turned back and saw Ruby staring at me.

"What happened Ruby?" I asked her, trying to calm my fast-beating heart!

"That's what I want to ask to you? What happened? Why are you still awake?"

"Nothing." I spoke harshly, giving her a hint that I was disinterested to talk to her.

"Is it Ranil dancing in your mind again?!"

"No, nothing like that. I must sleep now." Slightly pushing her aside, I made my way to the bed.

Trin trin trin trin... the 'snooze' and 'off alarm' options were waiting for me. Finally, I chose the 'off' option and pushed myself out of bed to get ready. Hearing my commotion, Ruby opened her eyes asking-

"Ruhani, you woke up so early? Where are you going?"

"Nowhere Ruby. Me and my classmates are going for an outing."

"Oh, that's great, enjoy then." Thankfully, she didn't ask me much questions. I was happy for that. Taking the warden's permission, I went out from the hostel building and waited for Rushil's arrival. Finally, after a few minutes I saw an open jeep with blaring horn, approaching towards me by overtaking other vehicles. He stopped his jeep near me and I sat on the front seat.

"Good morning, Ruhani."

"Good morning, Rushil. So, where are we going? Your idea has buzzed me completely."

"I knew it will excite you. I am taking you to a place that's even more beautiful than you."

"Ahmmm...." I started blushing listening to his words.

He was driving the vehicle at constant speed. When we were moving out from the city the vehicles running by our side were becoming less in number. The extramundane view of the way was enveloping me in an aura of positivity. The trees planted on either side of the road were making a hemispherical door-like structure above it. They were mingling with the surrounding greenery in the cold, wintry air. Butterflies colliding with my face made me feel like an angel. At last, Rushil abruptly stopped the jeep and told me to look on my left side. As I did so, I noticed that it was no less than a fairyland! The scenic view fascinated me so much that I took no time in jumping out of the jeep and rushing to the garden; a huge garden. The sun was amplifying its corn-coloured shine everywhere. The barks and branches of the trees were playing hide and seek with its light creating komorebi. The psithurism of the trees made me reach ecstasy. The garden had birds of various colours flitting around of and their medley with different species of flora & fauna made the whole milieu look so elegant. There were also white-coloured Cupid statues placed over the stage between a small pond. The whole environment thrilled me so much that I forgot about Rushil's presence. Till date, people had invited me to watch movies, to visit amusement parks, to eat at restaurants, but no one had ever made me see such a magnificent place. I still carry the spectacular views of that place in my heart. Enjoying with Mother Nature, I suddenly saw Rushil following me quietly. I ran towards him and exulted, "Thank you so much, Rushil! This place is amazing; I will never forget this surprise." Rushil was beaming at me. Seeing my pure elation, he remarked - "You are just like little child, Ruhani."

We both were ambling along a small stream. It was a man-made garden, specially made for green panthers. Only few people knew about it and one of them was Rushil.

"So Ruhani, did you like this place?" asked Rushil, taking out a chocolate from his pocket. "Very much". I replied quickly snatching the chocolate from him.

"Ruhani, I wanted to make this day memorable and this moment too."

"Which moment Rushil?" I asked. The next moment, he sat on his knees and spoke - "This moment."

Rushil's act dazed me. I was unable to react. I hadn't expected this at all. Noticing him searching for something in his pockets made my throat go dry. He took out a shiny thing; it was a ring. With a rainbow of hopes in his eyes and a beatific smile on his face he was looking at me, actually waiting for me to bring my hand forward. I did, but to make him stand.

"I am sorry, Rushil. I don't feel the same way as you feel for me." I spoke softly, unable to make eye contact with him. Rushil lowered his gaze. In the next moment he looked at me intensely, the anguish visible on his face. Without speaking a single word, he took out the keys to his jeep from his pocket and stepped forward to move out from the garden. "Come Ruhani, let's go." he said. I followed him and sat beside him wordlessly. He too drove the jeep without uttering anything in relation to my denial.

"Rushil, I hope you won't hold a grudge against me" I said stammering. I could understand the pain he was going through.

"Ruhani, don't be silly. Who thinks like this? We are still good friends; I can't force you to evoke feelings of love for me. Of course, it did hurt me, but forget it now." He was so calm when he spoke this. I felt bad for him. I grasped his suffering. He was in pain and was worse in hiding his emotions. But at last, I realized the hollowness of the biggest lie I was telling myself from so many years – "One day, I will move on."

On the way back, I kept wondering about my acts which were clearly showing that my behaviour with Rushil was matchless. Perhaps it was those acts that had prompted him to propose me. It wasn't Rushil's fault; it was mine. I had turned into an unfathomable person.

Rushil stopped the jeep and I got out of it. "Bye Rushil" - I said. His response was just a slight smile and nodding of the head.

"I lost him." I spoke to myself. At that moment I felt so empty. Yes, for a moment I thought of calling Rushil and say 'Yes' to him, but I wasn't sure. I sat in a nearby park repeatedly playing the reverse button of my mind. Over-thinking for a while, I traipsed to my room to see Ruby's annoying face.

Opening the door, she said- "So you are back! How was your outing? I did not see any girl with you when you were going out!" she commented in an accusatory tone.

"Please Ruby, I don't want you to interrogate me now. Do it later if you want to, but for now just leave me alone!" I shouted, throwing my bag on the bed.

Ruby was piqued by my attitude and kept to herself. After she got to know that Rushil remained my friend even after I had made them meet, her attitude towards me had turned toxic. Sometimes it looked like she was my true friend and sometimes I doubted this thought of mine. Whatever! Throwing her thoughts away and laying on the bed, I started thinking about the ideas which could make Rushil jovial again, but none of them seemed to be effective. Only my 'yes' would seem to work its magic, but I didn't want to say that. I had overused my mind. As a result, I felt the need of a tonic which could rejuvenate it. I opened the book which I had gotten issued. Reading about the author and introductory pages, I was about to read the first page but suddenly the book was snatched by Ruby.

"Ruby, is this the way you behave?! Give me my book back!" I screamed.

"No" she shouted, "I won't and never will."

"But what is your problem? And now please tell me the person's name who was changed by reading just a mere book."

"I can't."

"Ok then, return me my book."

We both were shouting at each other and squabbling like cats - something we never did before. I pushed her back and tried to grab the book but her hold over the book was so tight that I was unable to take it back. She then slapped me hard on my face. I got angry but meanwhile I realized the seriousness of the matter. "Ruby has never showed signs violence earlier, but now if she is doing this, then there must be a solid reason behind it." I thought.

"Ruby stop it. Speak to me clearly."

"Rushil......Rushil it was." She shouted. "He is the person who was changed! He is the person who got attracted towards the spirits. He can control these spirits, trap them. I warned you, Ruhani; he is not worthy of your friendship. He wears the mask of a glorified soul which never slips off publicly. I was his girlfriend to whom he had proposed, not any another girl who was chasing him. I was the one who left him. His madness for that Satanic work just increasing day by day. Finally, I detached myself from him. I could no longer live with a beelzebub" Ruby said, crying her heart out.

Whatever I was hearing, was hard to swallow. It was something unusual. I was stunned listening to her words. I wondered whether after using all possible strategies to separate me from Rushil, she was trying this weird way in a hope to get success?! "Ruby...come on! It's the 21st century. In 2003 itself, the Maharashtra government had introduced the anti-superstition bill."

"Yeah, I know and it became act in 2013. So?"

"But then too people like you try to make issues out of these trivial things. These things don't exist. It is only your psychology; maybe you were brainwashed."

"Listen Ruhani, I don't believe in black magic, sorcery, witchcraft or anything like that, but how can you deny the existence of spirits? It exists in you, it exists in me." she spoke confidently, looking deep into my eyes.

I did not have any answer to this question. I had never imagined these things. Though I it was trying my best to shield my mind from believing Ruby, but yeah somewhere her manipulation worked. I was horrified in my heart because Rushil did talk about ghosts and spirits. Well, actually, everyone does, but confronted by Ruby's claims, it made me doubt him. I was shivering while thinking of my past where I lived with conformist minds and now with a malevolent devil. Both were mingled together to horrify me. Both had the same goal - to snatch the liberty of people. I started lamenting over my situation. Ruby hugged me tightly and said, "Don't worry, everything will be alright. Don't cry, relax yourself dear. I know you still talk to him but you need to keep yourself away from him" she spoke caressing my head.

Thinking about how a woman can be the toughest rival of another woman, Anjali smirked. Alongside, she was also feeling pity for Ruhani for not understanding people's true intentions and easily getting influenced.

Ruhani continued- "It was 11:00 PM. Lying on the bed I was incessantly visualizing the consequences of disheartening Rushil which were striking me with horror, but I was unsure about the untested facts given by Ruby about him. Believing people easily had always been my weakness. "Maybe Ruby had spoken merely out of hatred." I thought. My continuously vibrating mobile phone distracted me from my thoughts. Its screen showed Rushil's name. I was not in mood to attend his call, not because of Ruby's short-lived manipulation but because of the guilt I was holding from the moment he had proposed to me.

I spent that entire night wondering about some bizarre things. On the same night I sent a mail to Ranil mentioning everything that had happened that day, including the way Rushil had proposed me. Becoming vulnerable in front of his emotions and feelings, eventually I ended up typing a really long mail.

Chapter 8
Moment of elation

Being heavy-eyed for hours I missed all my morning classes. Without even looking at Ruby, I packed my bag and got ready for attending the remaining classes. Walking towards the college, I decided to distance myself from Rushil. I was in fear and hoping that Rushil would not commit any felonious act to have me. Suddenly I saw a car in our campus approaching speedily in the direction where I was standing. Suddenly, it stopped few metres away from me. The dust which was playing a role of partial curtains between me and the car was fading slowly. The door of the car opened. I saw a man getting out from his ritzy shiny, red coloured vehicle. I rubbed my eyes and peered at him.

"You could have killed me, idiot!" I shouted running towards Rushil to hit him hard.

"No dear, I had no such intentions." He spoke with a chortle and started talking to me. When he was speaking, I saw another man coming out from that car. He banged the door and approached us. The dust was still dancing in the air. Through it, I was trying hard to identify him; somehow it seemed to be a familiar face. "Who is he? A friend of Rushil's?" I thought, I tried again. Finally, I was able to use my 563 mp gadget to see the man. He came near us and stood beside Rushil.

"Hi...I am Ranil." He spoke looking fixedly at me.

Rushil then introduced me to his brother Ranil. "Ruhani, he is my elder brother Ranil." As soon as I saw Ranil, I felt a thousand butterflies dancing in my stomach!!! All-consuming love once again set my soul on fire. Once more his charm bedazzled me. I was overloaded with euphoria. "He came back!" I spoke to myself. I gawked at them when I got to know that Ranil and Rushil were brothers. I spoke nothing. I just kept gazing at Ranil's mesmerizing eyes. From a mischievous boy, Ranil had turned into a fine gentleman. He had acquired a fit body with a clean-shaven face and a lopsided smile which I loved the most. He looked at me with the same passion as I beheld within my heart.

"And you know what Ruhani, he will soon be entering in the category of the top businessmen of our country!" said Rushil patting his brother's back proudly. I nodded my head and kept gazing at Ranil. Controlling my tears from rolling down, my heart experienced an ecstatic love by feeling the presence of its other half around it. I wanted to ask him so many questions! Where had he gone? What was he doing? Why had he come back so late? But I asked nothing because his attitude showed that he was well-heeled man now.

"Ruhani... Helloo... Ruhani...I know he is a slayer by looks, but I had misunderstanding of considering you too hard to be pleased. You even rejected me!"

Rushil's words made me realize my lunatic behaviour. I looked at him with a smiling face. "Ohh! It's nothing like that Rushil. If someone or something is good, they should be adored" I said looking at Ranil. He smirked hearing my words.

"Yes, you are right." Rushil answered with a laugh. Promptly we heard some voices coming closer. I saw some girls coming near us.

"Hey Rushil, who is he? A new admission in the end of the session? Hahaha." Saying this, those four girls started chuckling at their own tedious joke.

"He is my brother and by grasping your intention I want to say that - he is least interested in anyone of you." Rushil spoke with moroseness, proudly looking at his brother.

"Rushil, your dogmatic mind can only reach to a substandard level We had no such intentions. It is better you keep your assumptions with yourself." One of the girls roared and then all of them walked away.

Rushil was shocked. Though he had shown such brusqueness to those girls in the past, but none of them had talked to him like that earlier. Maybe it was the time for revenge as the session was at its end. The situation turned awkward. Ranil and I were standing quiet, giving each other a weird look. Rushil noticed both of us and laughed loudly. "Hahahaha ...that was terrible!" he said. Ranil and I understood the fake-ness in his laugh, but we too accompanied him by laughing and created more awkwardness.

I was happy to stumble across Ranil. Add to that, another happy thing for me was that - Rushil was behaving utterly fine as if nothing had happened. I was mistaken for portraying him as a rogue. "Ok Ranil, let's go and take a round of the campus" he said and took Ranil with him. I was staring at Ranil till he faded away from the scene. I smiled, looked up at the sky and thought "Was this real? Has he come back to be with me? Or is it just a coincidence?" God's plan was still a mystery. I looked at that red book and advanced towards the library.

Returning the book to the librarian I requested him to not to make this book issuable anymore. He gave me a harsh look with his big eyes while adjusting his spectacles. I headed back to my room, threw myself on the bed and kept thinking about the scenario on a loop. A vexatious question in my mind was throwing me into panic - "Does Ranil still loves me?" I was brooding over the question when the buzz of my mobile phone interrupted me. I looked on the screen which was displaying an unknown number.

"Hello, who is this?"

"Aaaaa...your eternal love!"

"Ranil..." I whispered.

"Huh..." he sighed and added, "I am happy to know that you are able to recognise my voice."

"And I am shocked to know that this kind of thought erupted in your mind at all!" I chided. There was a brief silence, wherein we only heard each other's breath.

I wanted to berate him for his ignorant behaviour, fight with him but soon realised that the best option was just to ignore him. But, as I kneeled down, I melted. Why was I not able to hold my grudge? I still think about it sometimes.

My list of questions was ready to be answered, but he chose a coffee shop where the examination was to be conducted. We decided to meet at the cafe which was not known to much people.

"Oh, so you forgave him!" Anjali asked with a shocked expression, finding Ruhani's decision based on emotion rather than intelligence. She was thinking about Ruhani's past with Ranil where she wasn't at all treated the way she deserved.

"Undoubtedly! I always knew he was my twin flame. I agree, he did commit some mistakes in past, but now, certainly he had come with some plans of stability. The next day I reached 'The Isolated Cafe' sharp at 6:00 P.M. True to its name, it looked totally isolated. The mammoth hall had walls embellished with different coffee quotation posters, along with some round tables having similar posters pasted on it. One of the posters with a white background had a small message that said - "Come, lets revive our memories." Reading the line, I stood still for few seconds, thinking about Ranil's imminent arrival. I felt my heartbeat throbbing in anticipation. Regaining control over my overwhelming emotions, I looked around and abruptly collided with an awkward moment after seeing a couple sitting in a corner holding each other's hand with their legs twisted under the table.

The cafe had three waiters dressed formally with a cute black bow at their neck. Two of them were looking at me with eagerness to take the order, and the third one having squeaky clean face was leering at the couple especially the lady. He seemed quite creepy. The awkwardness in the milieu made me feel a bit uncomfortable, but on the whole, the place was serene. I chose a table beside the window. Waiting for Ranil, I kept entangling my fingers with each other nervously. Tired of the activity, I started looking out, feasting my eyes on the pinkish blue sky with the red sun fading away, making a cluster of sparrows fly to their homes. Some of them sat on the red bottle brush tree, planted near the window. The frisky sparrows gliding on the twigs caused a scarlet rain of flower spikes, which sprinkled on the ground like saffron. My mind's tumult was blowing over. Simmering down, I glittered and heaved a sigh of relief observing the ethereal surroundings.

"Ma'am here's the menu." Handing over cafe's handmade menu, the waiter hurriedly ran to the kitchen on the chef's call.

"Tune oh rangeele kaisa jaadu kiya…

… piya piya bole matwala jiya."

An old melody of early 80's was unfurling its magic in the cafe. I was grooving to the music but my impatient eyes were constantly looking at the door. Continuously checking my watch, I could feel my right leg shaking out of twitchiness. 30 minutes passed but Ranil was still missing. A negative thought spewed in my mind and started creating a mess in it - "Will he come, or he is just taking me for granted as always? He knows I still love him; is he just playing with my feelings to make himself feel the desired one?" But the scenario I anticipated soon evaporated in thin air as soon as I saw the man approaching me.

I stood up to greet Ranil, continuously blinking my eyes. Somewhere he too must have experienced discomfiture. Shaking my hand with a slight smile we comforted ourselves on the hardwood Adirondack chairs. Keeping his hands on the table Ranil asked - "So, how are you?"

"Umm... all well, everything is going great."

"Okay, so you were relishing the moments without me, isn't it?" sneering he threw a jibe at me.

Piqued by his words, my hemming and hawing melted away in an instant! I flared up and yelled, "Was it me or you who left first? Where were you gone?" My voice became harsh while asking him those questions. He looked at me and warmly spoke - "Ruhani, listen. I am sorry, for whatever I did. I know my way was wrong or totally insane, but I wasn't able to deny what I felt for you. I tried hard not to come into your life again. I felt insecure whenever you mentioned about the boys who proposed to you; including Rushil."

"So, you did read my emails then?!" shockingly I asked.

"Yes, I did. Each and every mail. Ruhani, I had feelings for you, but it was my self-seeking act to walk with a safe side; that's why I distanced myself from you. But your memories always scratched my heart. Though I was wrapped up in my frenetic schedule but during the stillness of the dark and dingy nights, my heart screeched only your name. I wanted to contact you but lacked pluckiness to face your questions and you as well. I was wallowing in a pool of guilt. Then, I got to know about your condition and that made me feel like an even bigger culprit. Ironically, it was difficult for me to come back as all your sufferings were because of me. Also, I had a lot of fear. We belonged to such opposite backgrounds; I was sure that the conclusion would be nothing but our separation."

"Ranil, why don't you agree that you lacked guts to hold my hand?! There are many couples out there who belong to different culture but are standing together to face this world."

"Yes, I was not gutsy, I agree. But this is real life; not a movie where we turn ourselves into rebels - try to understand that. I needed to do something exceptional to spend my whole life with you, and now I can bet that my success will not allow our families to counter us. Do you think it was a facile task to leave you like that? I know it hurt you tremendously. I know it was an unendurable journey, but it was all for you." He paused and held my hand tenderly, making me believe that he deeply regretted whatever he did. The way he spoke, melted the solid crust which concealed the feeling of love in my heart for so many years.

"Will you leave me again if the feeling of love gets replaced with self-love?" I spoke softly with moist eyes, looking at him without blinking.

"Ruhani, I never felt the same way for anyone else as I felt for you. Night and day, I strived to move on. Soon I realised that I wanted to be with you; our compatibility was miraculous. Yes, I ran from you when I got to know that you belong to a different religion. I bended backwards to suppress my feelings which were arousing for you without a pause. But fortuitously, my every attempt proved futile. I was obstinately determined to give our relation a tight bond, but reality shook me, and I stepped back. At that point of time whatever I found right, I did. My dear... I apologise for that. Sincerely." He maintained his soft tone to speak, his every word was worth to be heard with grok. In spite of that, I showed him a fake termagant side of mine.

"Ranil, because of your phobia I suffered so much that you can't even imagine! And what if I would have fallen for someone else?" I asked slapping the table-top furiously.

"Listen Ruhani..."

"Hello ma'am, your order please" the waiter interrupted Ranil disturbing him and me as well.

Ranil hastily opened the menu card and said – "Two cappuccinos." He gave the order by reading the name of the first beverage written on the menu.

"Thank you, sir" the waiter said looking at Ranil in a strange way and went off.

"Well, I never thought about it. I was suffering in the inferno, and somewhere I knew you were suffering too. Your emails were proof of that. Our bond was crystallized. Initially I wanted you to go with someone else; later it all changed."

"During these past five years, did you never get involved with anyone? I thought you must have, as you became uncertain about me. You feared whether I would bury the hatchet or not. You were and you are a milksop, Ranil!" I must have sounded vitriolic to him but the outrage I was showing didn't had any connection with the feelings within me, as every word he spoke was true.

My words triggered his shady side. Looking straight to my face he growled - "I am not here to listen to this bullshit of doubting a man who came here just for you! I worked extremely hard to achieve everything on my own steam, just to be with you. And what am I getting? Doubts? If you don't want to be with me then I can very well leave again." I knew I was making a mistake by asking him irrelevant questions. I should not have done that. After all, he had returned for me.

Sensing the sensitivity of the situation I lowered my voice and spoke with moist eyes - "But you never tried to know my condition. I was dying everyday thinking that you never cared and never will. Is this the way you are going to treat me after we come together?"

"Ruhani, I was always concerned about you."

"No, you were never. I went through the hell which you can't even imagine. Don't give me ludicrous reasons. I was suffering tremendously, Ranil. Your one act of kindness could have solved the problem, but you kept yourself away from me just because a sense of foreboding had made home in your heart."

"Ruhani, at that time I was doubtful about our togetherness. I didn't want to make ourselves addicted to each other. Also, I never wanted you to become vulnerable without me. One is never sure about the future. Today I am sitting with you but if in the next moment I am gone forever, then that attachment will make you suffer a lot."

"Ranil, I did experience that, but the point is you never cared."

"I did. Who do you think Ozil was? Why was your treatment non-identical from the other patients?"

"I mentioned about Ozil in my emails, but how are you reason for making him treat me differently?" I was perplexed listening to him.

"He became my friend when Rohit introduced me to him. He was Rohit's cousin. He proved to be a very good friend of mine" Ranil said with a sigh.

"What?" I was shocked listening to those unexpected words.

"Yes, and Rohit is also our mutual friend. He kept this fact hidden from you on my behest."

Ranil was revealing some deep secrets which I had never thought of at all. I questioned myself about the quality of the man. His friends, who were also my friends, never told me anything about Ranil in spite of knowing everything. They were so loyal to him. But I clutched his weakness of being fearful. He created an image of his in my mind of being a personality who would never dare to take decisions independently. Thinking about societies, cultures, people beyond a certain limit surely wreaks havoc on our lives, and kills us from within every day.

While talking to him, one thing which alarmed my mind was the reason behind Ozil's suicide.

"Ranil, do you know the reason why Ozil ended his life like that? He was a psychiatrist! What drained him out to this extent?" I asked.

"It might have been his loneliness" Ranil said keeping his eyes still.

"Yes, many a times he seemed to be coated by loneliness while remembering his beloved wife."

"Ozil was not just an excellent psychiatrist but also a praiseworthy human being. Rohit informed me about your aggravating condition and your mails too made me very worried. To rejuvenate you, he talked to me about Dr Ozil. I was convinced that Ozil was the only person who had the power to bring you back to life. I asked Rohit to recommend Ozil to your family. Rohit did full justice to the work given to him, and so did Ozil" Ranil spoke holding my hand tenderly.

"But my dear, why Dr. Ozil? Your arrival could have pulled me out of that condition in a moment. Be frank, you didn't want to come to me."

"Yes, yes! I didn't want to come! Okay? How many times do I have to say that?!" Ranil screamed getting agitated.

The next few moments passed in silence. Then slowly, Ranil continued, "One day Rohit called and informed me about the Ozil's suicide. I was not at all ready to believe him. Rohit also apprised that the police needed my help in investigation. It took me a few days to come back to Jodhpur."

"Oh, do you know anything about his letter?"

"Which letter?" he spoke in confoundment, as if he did not have any idea about that letter.

"His suicide letter, Ranil!"

"Oh, yeahh...I remember now. The letter is still with the police. They inquired about his death and claimed it to be a murder. They did their inquiry; I was included in it. Eventually they found no evidence of murder and it was considered a suicide" said Ranil slowly sipping his coffee.

"They inquired about his suicide from my parents and me too. But were you not stupid for still not confronting me? You can never understand how I felt after losing Ozil. I wanted you to be with me, I was all alone that time."

"Ruhani, stop it, I came here for you. I feel sorry for whatever happened with Ozil. Who are we to control people and situations? We cannot do anything beyond our capacity."

"But Ranil...Ozil was my close friend. I knew him very well. He was not a pusillanimous man. Such kind of a poltroonish act can never be his choice. He loved his life. Come on, he was a psychiatrist! Don't you think it's illogical to consider it a suicide?"

"Enough! I think I should leave now. If you can bring Ozil back, then go; bring him. I don't know why he committed suicide or whatever. Ruhani, you are over thinking." Ranil spoke getting flustered. "I came here for you; I want to marry you. Now, forget all these grisly incidents, and think about the present. The future. Our future."

"Hmmm, sorry for over-reacting. Tell me one thing - are you sure about your feelings now? Regarding me?"

"What kind of a question is that? Obviously, I am. Please Ruhani, I have realized my mistake. The uncertainty is gone. I won't go away this time. Please stop this. I am here to make you mine."

"Ranil....I was always yours." Holding his hands, overwhelmed with emotions of love, I said, kissing the palms of his hands. When I lifted my head, a drop of tear fell on his palm bedecking its half-moon.

He blushed; also coated with guilt, he uttered- "It was unexpected, Ruhani. I never thought you will forgive me. Thank you so much, my love. Oh, by the way, I heard that you are Rushil's best friend. I think he likes you very much. I saw your pictures on Facebook with him."

"Oh...were you on Facebook? I searched for you many times. Why were you not visible to me?"

"I had deactivated my all accounts. I came back on these sites only a few months ago. I haven't come here to meet Rushil. I came for you, because I found it to be the right time."

"Right time? You were reading my mails, right? Maybe the news of him proposing to me bewildered you?"

"No, I planned for this visit months ago. Tell me one thing, do you like Rushil?"

"Yes, I do. He possesses so many good qualities."

"Hmm… definitely he possesses many good qualities, but I want him to improve himself in connection with girls. His friends told me that he is a playboy. I didn't want to tell you this, but since sooner or later you are going to be a part of my family it was essential to disclose this secret."

"I don't think so, Ranil. He is my dear friend. I have been with him for almost two years."

"Don't forget he is my brother; I know him and his habits better."

"Is that so? Well then, I don't think you know even inch of him." When I said this, Ranil's face became blank; his disinterest was visible. To change his mood, I quickly switched my question and continued "So did he tell you anything about me?"

"Nothing much… but I am happy to know that there is at least one person who could become a medium of affection between me and Rushil."

"Don't you love your brother Ranil?"

"Of course, I do! But he could never understand me. He should understand that whatever I and our parents speak is for his own betterment. Well, I know that once he gets to know about us, he will be the first person to tell us that we should tie the knot as soon as possible."

"No... Ranil... don't tell anyone about us so early. Please! I know, you are successful now, but still, we have differences. Firstly, we should have a civil marriage; then we can have a grand reception."

"Okay.... that's not a bad idea. A secret wedding."

"No, not a secret wedding, but just a ceremony with only close ones - my parents and your family, I mean your parents, because I don't know how will Rushil react?"

"Oh, look Ruhani, I want you to talk about us to your parents but I can't tell my parents. They are not easy to convince; they will take time. It's better to have cordial relations with good-hearted people. But more than all of that, currently, you should focus on your exams. Hopefully, I will marry you soon. Now we have our own house. I have purchased a flat in Sukoon Apartments. I showed your picture to the secretary of that apartment and his family. They liked you a lot. Mr Das's family will surely treat you like their own family member" Ranil said, kissing my hand. I glittered. That smile which came on my face wiped out all my tears which flowed every night remembering him.

*

The next day Rushil took me and Ranil to Sky Beach. Looking for a place to sit, he told Ranil about his birthday when I gave him a small party at this place. Mentioning the gifts that I had given him, Rushil looked at me with a beaming face. But when I looked at Ranil, I found his visage to be bitter. He had a wide smile on his face but his eyes were telling a distinctively opposite story.

"Ruhani, you sit here" Rushil spoke suddenly, making me sit on a corner seat touching the wall and seating himself beside me. Ranil looked at me with squinted eyes. With a quick sigh, he lifted his eyebrows in a way that it looked like a silent taunt. The whole scenario made his face taut.

"Hey Ranil, you must try sweet potato burritos here. They are fantastic! Ruhani, you remember that day, how many times I thanked you for ordering that dish?"

"Yeah, I remember." Uttering this I again looked at Ranil. He was busy fiddling with his phone without reacting to what Rushil was saying.

From ordering the dishes to finishing our meal, I experienced waves after waves of Ranil's silent rage. Continuously conveying his rage through his eyes, he made me feel guilty every second. I realised that my closeness with Rushil was not going to be digested by Ranil so easily. Paying the bill, and making effort to stand keeping his palms on his thighs he smiled at both of us and spoke "Thank you for this wonderful feast, but sorry, I won't be able to join you further. I think you both should carry on with your fun activities. I need to go on an urgent basis. I hope you won't mind."

"Oh!! Is that so? It's okay, don't worry" Rushil retorted breezily. Then he turned to me and said with a flourish, "After you Ma'am." His gesture increased the sensation of fear in me. I was sweating seeing Ranil burning inside.

Clicking the unlock button of his car, Ranil sat in it. "Okay Rushil, see you soon, sorry again."

"Please Ranil, we both are okay."

"Hmm... I can see that. Fine, see you after I finish my work. Bye..." he said driving away swiftly.

"Woahh… Ranil has started driving really fast. I never saw him like this before. He is such a changed man. I am happy Ruhani. It seems now I will finally be experiencing my family's love. Finally, a happy family."

What was I supposed to say now? None of them told me detailed version of their story. Their relation with each other literally confused me.

"Ruhani, look there, an auto. Let's go." Holding my hand Rushil said, escorting me to the auto. We crossed the road hand-in-hand. At that moment, I involuntarily compared Rushil with Ranil, and Rushil seemed to be well-disposed than his brother. Anxiety struck me when I found myself trapped between the two. No doubt, I was still Ranil's, but his boorish behaviour flared a fire in me, which in turn sparked a comparison between the two.

Looking out from the auto rickshaw Rushil seemed to be relishing the ride. We were going ahead without uttering a single word. Rushil asked the auto driver to stop in front of Nehru Garden, a park near to our college.

"Looking at Ranil being so serious about his work makes me realise why he succeeded so much in just a few years. He is an awesome businessman!" Rushil exulted, keeping the change given by rickshaw driver in his wallet.

"Rushil, can I ask you something? Promise you won't take it otherwise."

"Oh, come on! I won't, and you know that."

"Hmm, I wanted to ask you... don't you have any complaints from your family now?"

He turned his head towards me, and answered calmly - "No, I don't. I mean it's okay. For how long will I carry grudges against my own family? My brother has come to visit me. He was so happy to see me. I was craving for this kind of love from my family, and they have finally gifted me that."

Looking at him I noticed his innocence. A seven-year long grudge only needed a small act of warmth to diminish. During those two years, I had never heard Rushil speaking about his family - not even hateful words. Albeit, sometimes it was clearly visible on his face that he missed them a lot.

*

At night standing on the balcony, I was admiring the effulgent stars. Plugging in my earphones I played – "Toote hue khwabon se, humne ye jaana hain."

Losing myself into the classic melody I mused over my relationship with Ranil. Taking a deep breath, I looked down and mumbled, "I am happy he came back, but he is indecisive. What if he changes his mind again?"

Suddenly the song I was playing was interrupted by a vibration. Pulling out the mobile phone from my pyjama pockets I read the name - 'Ranil'. I answered his call but stood wordlessly.

"Hello...Hello! Ruhani!?"

"Hmm..."

"Are you still angry at me?" he asked in a gravelly voice.

"What do you think?"

"You are."

"Then what is the sense in asking?"

"I am sorry for my behaviour; I don't why was I envying Rushil's generosity towards you. I felt like he cares for you a lot or probably still loves you in spite of your denial. I think you should not have kept cordial relations with him."

"Ranil, I can handle it. You should control your emotions. If he still loves me then it is his concern.

Why are you ruffled by his behaviour? I waited for you for so long and you are still doubting my loyalty towards you?!"

"No, never Ruhani! I am not doubting your loyalty at all. I just love you, that's why."

"Tell me, is getting possessive or insecure validates that you love me?"

Ranil kept quiet when I asked him this question. I felt strung out watching him behave in such a weird manner. If he knew me well, if he trusted me, then what was the sense behind observing Rushil's behaviour whose proposal I had denied before his arrival?

Ranil apologised to me again, and promised to never steer his mind into the zone of insecurity.

As soon as he disconnected the call, I received a call from Rushil. I didn't want to talk to him at that moment, may be because I had judged him for playing the role of a barrier in my and his brother's relation. Nevertheless, I finally I did attend his call.

"Hi Ruhani, what's going on?" He asked while eating something.

"Nothing, I was listening to a song…"

"Oh! Which song?"

"Toote hue khwabon se, humne ye jaana hain" I said in a dreary voice, so as to give him a hint about my unwillingness to talk. It slipped from my mind that the person who I was talking was Rushil. He wouldn't disconnect the call till he brought me back to my sunny disposition.

"God! Why do you hear such dirge? I am sure you are not from this era! There are so many fresh melodies out there. Why don't you hear those?"

"Rushil, no one is denying you to listen those songs. Better you don't speak in the matter of my choice, and please stop behaving like a creep! You are my friend and as your friend, I am advising you to have some self-respect. I know you still feel for me, but you need to understand the reality." I was churlish to speak without caring much about his feelings. I think my unruly craze for Ranil made me do that.

"Oh... yeah... right, I need to understand. Do you know even yourself well, Ruhani? I don't think so you are aware of your inner voice. I hope one day you will achieve clarity of thoughts. Then, you won't see me as a burden. But till that happens, I won't disturb you henceforth. So, bye." He replied with a pause, his voice going low after each line. Rushil's reply made me shiver! What did he mean by saying, 'he won't disturb me'? I know, he was hurt. He must have never thought that I would talk to him as if he didn't mean anything to me. But he was too quick to take the decision of saying goodbye too early and so easily.

"Rushil...Rushil..." I cried out, but the call got disconnected. I kept ringing his phone continuously but he didn't attend any of my calls. Oh God! The heaviness I felt was unmatchable when compared to every heart-wrenching incident that had happened in my life thus far. Silently crying, I cursed Rushil for not being sensitive enough to understand me. Failing to control my emotions, my rage reached mountains, consequently making me send him text messages full of abomination which were meant to humiliate him at its best. Shocking fact was that he didn't reply to any of my messages.

It was the last day when I heard Rushil's voice. He never called me back, neither did I try to contact him.

*

What next? That was still a mystery. Life was giving me so many surprises at each step. One more surprise came to me, as well as to all other students, was the final exams getting preponed. Everyone was ready to join the race. Examinations seemed to play havoc but our power of fighting with exams was at its paramount.

The days passed swiftly in the blink of an eye. Now it was time for each and every outsider to pack their bags and return to the place they belonged to. My luggage was ready to reach the final destination. At one point, I saw the warden ma'am approaching towards me with a smile on her face. Softly pinching my cheek, she said, "Take care, dear child." Doing the same to Ruby, she waved and left to meet other girls.

Ruby and I came out from the hostel building and for the last time, gazed back at the college campus, reminiscing about all the moments spent there. My eyes teared up. Suddenly, we heard the sound of horns blowing loudly. Realizing that Ranil was waiting for us in his car we both rushed towards him at full speed. Looking at us he guffawed and came running towards us. He took our luggage and kept it in his car. Ruby seemed discomposed at that time, and the reason was unknown. Driving slowly Ranil played a beautiful song by One Republic -

'But baby I been, I been prayin' hard,

said no more counting dollars

We'll be counting stars.'

I smirked at Ranil listening to the lyrics; he winked at me with impish smile. Feeling shy I looked back to see Ruby's reaction. She was glaring at me! It was too galling. Not caring much about her, I started talking to Ranil.

"Ranil, where is Rushil? Have you told him about us?" I spoke doubting that he must have revealed everything.

"Ruhani, I don't know exactly. He must be in his flat."

"Ohh... okay" I replied, grasping that the relation between the two still lacked the syrupy bridge connecting them.

Reaching the railway station Ruby jumped out. Getting her luggage, she uttered a hasty "bye" and scuttled off to her train, while we both were still sitting in the car.

"Is she really your friend?" Ranil asked, making a weird face at me.

"Umm...Earlier she was. Presently... I don't know." I spoke keeping my head down.

"Shirley is irreplaceable. Where is she?"

"Must be busy with her goals. I am not in touch with her since the last three months."

"Oh, don't worry, she will be back" Ranil said, kissing my hand.

"Yeah, I know. Like you are back, she will be too." Giggling I looked in the rear-view mirror wiping the extra kohl from my eye. Ranil got out of the car. Unlocking the boot of the car, he took out my luggage. I could hear his 'Aaaarghh' when he was pulling out the load.

"Are we ready to go?" he asked coming near my window. Gulping, I stepped out of the car with a heavy heart. Crossing the path, main gate and security check, we now were standing on platform no. 5. The hustle-bustle on the platform gave me a headache. I took out a Crocin from my purse. Searching for my water bottle, I unchained all my bags, but found nothing. Ranil was watching me standing beside. Asking me to chain the bags properly he headed towards a small shop and bought me a water bottle.

Gulping the medicine, I thanked Ranil. Suddenly a push from behind threw me on his chest. He covered me with his arms to protect me from falling but I quickly stepped back feeling shy. My train was late; so Ranil and I sat on a bench holding each other's hand.

"So Ruhani, what's next?"

"I don't know, you should guide me for that."

"Ruhani, I want you to tell everything to your parents. I will be coming to Jodhpur after two days. I need to go Gurugram, and after that I want to meet your parents."

"Ranil, don't you feel panicky pondering over this thorny path?"

"My love, I won't repeat the same mistake I committed seven years ago. Assuming and over-thinking will only lead to desolation. I don't want to mull over the consequences. Be by my side, that's enough" spoke tightly holding my hand in a gesture of assurance.

"But I am afraid to confess in front of my parents. How will I? They believe that their daughter will never do anything against their will."

"Hehe, did my spirit enter into yours?" He said poking me in the stomach. "Listen, we all love our parents Ruhani, but it doesn't mean we become puppets in their hands. They think about our best, but they are humans too. Many a times, they become illogical too. Listen, I am not trying to bulldoze you. Whenever you feel ready to divulge this information, do it. But

I cannot give you up this time. I will come to your parents and convince them for our marriage."

"And what if they deny?"

"Then I will wait for their positive response" he replied positively, caressing my hairs.

"For how long?"

"One year, two years, three years, or for my whole life! I cannot imagine my future with someone else, Ruhani. I want this beautiful damsel to become the mother of my children. I don't want anyone else."

I chortled gazing at him and sang, -"Tu mera kaun laage?"

"Ahann... I guess... your eternal love." He replied winking at me.

"You are my 'eternal love'." I replied. Then, in a trembling voice I uttered - "I love you Ranil."

He beamed and caressed me again.

"Mitegi na fir bhi mohabbat hamari, mitaane ke sau-sau bahaane banengai.

tumhein cheenale meri baahon se koi, mera pyaar yu besahara nahi hai.

Mera pyaar wo hai ke, marke bhi tumko juda apni baahon se hone na dega."

He crooned the same old song, which he used to sing for me many years ago.

"Just because I sang a song, was it mandatory for you to sing too?" I teased and embraced him heartily, observing, that the man possessed stout-heartedness and rectitude.

"I can't believe it! How can you forget this song? I always sang this song for you when we were together. Don't you remember?" Ranil asked.

"Ranil, do you think that's even possible?! I would play this song whenever I missed, listening to it sitting alone with your memories" I said softly. "But tell me, during those agonizing years which song was on loop in your play list?"

Without taking much time he sang- 'Toote hue khwabo ne, humko ye sikhaaya hai, dil ne, dil ne jise paayaa tha, aankhon ne gavaayaa hai.'

When his lips started twitching while singing, I stopped him clutching his wrist.

"I don't want to lose you Ruhani" he whispered with closed eyes.

Ranil had the guts to approach my parents; but I was uncertain. Even though he was using sugar-coated words, what if his heart again gets gripped with anxiety and fear? As for me, I wanted to marry him, but before that I wanted to gain a PhD in political science.

"What happened Ruhani?" he asked. I didn't answer him. He asked me again, but before I could reply, the train whistled. We both ran speedily to put the luggage in. Everything was kept properly. Ranil sat beside me and continued to guide me. After sometime the train whistled again; this time the call was for departure. Ranil stepped out from the train. I was looking at him through the window.

"Take care Ruhani, call me when you reach."

When the train started moving, I waved at Ranil with a Botox smile. I didn't want to say good-bye to him. As the train was increasing the distance amid us, the feelings of being separated from him again bounced back, covering my heart with agony. I saw the same pain on his face. My heart became restless. I tried to peep out from the train's window continuously just to unwind my eyes, which were starving for one glance of his before he totally disappeared from the scene. Ranil waved at me till I was visible to him. Then came a moment when we both faded away from each other's view. I engulfed my painful feelings and slunk on the seat with restless heart.

Chapter 9
Another fleeting heaven

After completing the five-hour journey wondering about my future with Ranil, I reached my city, my home, and my family, who were waiting for me on the platform - especially my father. The Ranthambore express stopped at platform no. 3. I hauled my bags as fast as I could. Me and my co-passengers were jostling to find the way out. Stoppage at a station definitely plays the role of an undeclared wrestling competition.

I leapt out with my luggage. Setting my feet on the platform I found myself encircled by people who were sweating to enter in. Again, I fought a war to break the human barricade. Dragging my bags to the platform I looked around for my family. Suddenly my eyes caught some creeps staring at me. One of them was stroking his lips with his thumb, sneering as if he owes me. Ignoring them, I walked ahead and took my mobile phone out from the purse. I opened my recent call logs and saw six missed calls from my father's number. Disquieted after seeing the missed calls I quickly dialled his number. Now he was the one who wasn't picking up the call. I kept ringing his phone continuously but got no response. After a while someone kept a hand on my shoulder from behind. Frightened I turned around and saw my father standing there. Bouncing in elation, I embraced him, squeezing him like a teddy bear! For a moment I was absorbed in thoughts of Ranil. But this musing was brushed away as soon as my father stroked my hair tenderly and kissed my forehead.

My mother was standing besides, with a glowing face. The radiance on her face could actually make one forget her sorrows. Welcoming me and keeping my head on her shoulders she kissed my cheek, "Finally you are with us, I am so happy!" she mumbled, but her silence and wet eyes were indicating something else. My arrival was a tear-jerking moment for my parents. Contrarily for me, the moment of departing from the railway station where I had left my beloved alone, was poignant.

 Keeping my luggage inside the car, we drove to our residence. When we arrived to our home, I asked my mother to hand over the keys to me, "The door is open" she said.

"What? Why? Is someone in the house?" Without waiting for her response, I darted towards the house full of beans, hoping for the presence of people with whom I had shared fond memories. Grinning I entered in, and bended, keeping both my hands on my knees. The next instant, I raised my head to see all my well-wishers assembled there! Even though I was hoping for exactly the same scenario, the shock I felt when it actually manifested, swept across my face swiftly. In anguish, I saw some of my relatives sitting inside the living room who were actually never my people. I greeted them with a not-so-great enthusiasm; they did the same. The animus in their eyes was clearly visible. I didn't want to sit with those people who transfer negative waves to you without a break. I found it wiser to walk silently into my room.

After a few minutes my father summoned me – "Ruhani, come beta, they all have come to meet you and you are hiding in your room. Come out and sit with us." Sluggishly getting up from my bed, I followed his order. Deliberately making loud click-clacking sound with my bedroom slippers, I stepped into the living room and sat with my father holding his hand. This was a major inappropriate behaviour for the people sitting there, and I tried my best to portray myself as spoiled child.

My bua(paternal aunt) glared at me, and fluffing her nostrils remarked - "Don't you think education brings prejudice in people, making them think as if they own this world?"

"No bua, I don't think so. It actually makes us break the walls of fake customs and traditions made by this society for their benefit." Startled with my sentence, they all started blathering about their ill-founded traditions. Suddenly, I interrupted my relatives to crack a joke which offended them. The joke was - "India possesses two types of people. First are the 'samajhdaar' (understanding and intelligent people) and second are the 'rishtedaar' (relatives)." It wasn't funny really, but yes, indirectly I had spoken my heart out through it. Listening to the joke they all advised me not to be facetious. My father was surely disappointed with my behaviour as he told me repeatedly to leave the place and help my mother in the kitchen. Being stubborn, I stayed there, but then got exasperated with their gossip. So, I left and walked to the kitchen for helping my mother.

Seeing me standing near the sink, my mother said, "Ruhani, I will do it. You should go and take rest."

"No Maa... let me help you." I smiled at her. She looked at me with tears in her eyes.

"What happened Maa?" I asked.

"Nothing dear, you will leave this house soon. Your aunt has brought a message from your in-laws. They want their son to get married now. They knew that if they will directly talk to your father, his answer would be no. Hence, they have asked your aunty to convince him."

Anjali was listening quietly, but she broke her silence on this statement. "What was your reaction then?"

Ruhani replied, "Well, obviously I was disheartened, but then I asked my mother about what Papa had to say about all this?" She said, "You know it very well, Ruhani. He won't go against his family's decision."

"Maa...I don't want to marry him. I don't like him!" I said kneeling down with wet eyes.

"Ruhani.... My dear, if I had power in my hands, I would have never allowed any one to interfere in my daughter's life. For me, the happiness of my child is the first priority. But I am helpless! You have to marry him. You don't have any option. We love you very much but please try to understand. I can't go against your father's will and your father can't break the prestige of his family."

"Am I his daughter or a goat to be sacrificed in the name of prestige?! If he loves me so much, why is he doing this?" I shouted and ran away to my room.

Locking the door I started lamenting my fate. I was mourning not only over my situation but for all those girls who are forced to tie the knot against their will, just to preserve the honour of their family. Pessimism engulfed me, making me unsure about my future with Ranil. None of them present in the living room noticed me as they were busy talking about the people who brought disgrace to their family by marrying a person of different culture. Their talks always sickened me. My mother didn't come after me as she didn't want to create any kind of scene.

"Ruhani... Where are you? Come fast, dinner is ready. See, every dish has prepared according to your choice" shouted my father.

I was angry with my father and wanted to take no notice of his call, but my love for him impelled me to obey him. Somehow, I regained my strength, washed my face, and went out for dinner. Everyone present there were talking about their fake splendid lifestyle. I sat beside my father and sneered at their stupid talks.

"Look dear, there are so many dishes" said my father treating me like a small child. Not in a mood to speak anything, I simply smiled at him.

While having dinner my father asked me about my plan for the PhD.

"And what about her marriage?!" bua interrupted rudely. "That boy is growing old, and so is this girl. Don't allow her to cross all limits. What will she do by studying further? She hasn't achieved anything yet, in spite of studying for so many years. In the end, she has to give birth to her husband's children. Even her in-laws won't allow her to earn. They have abundant property under their possession."

My father loved me the most, but many a times he became impotent when the person who belonged to his roots uttered their opinions in relation to me and my life. Whether it was bad or good, he just knew to obey them. I always wondered, why he did he always keep quiet? Why he was not able to speak up? What was the reason behind his acquiescence? That day also I pondered over the same questions. He should have answered bua that 'My daughter will not walk on the road you have planned for her. She will brace herself, and choose what is best for her. She is not an animal who will be chained up in the name of honour.' But he didn't. That was heartbreaking for me. I tried to understand his situation. Everything was giving me a sign that I must alter my personality from sturdy to sturdiest to make things happen and trust the Almighty.

Late at night I gave a call to Ranil and told him everything that had happened after reaching home. I also advised him to delay the idea of marriage as I wanted to work on my PhD. Regrettably, everything was heard by my aunt who was standing near my room. She created a scene shouting loudly all over the house. In bewilderment, my parents came running out from their room and asked, "What happened?"

"See?! This is the result of educating a girl!" bua taunted. I was shocked! Which result? Result of possessing independent thinking? Result of being honest to my parents by deciding to tell them everything? But none of them reached the level to conclude this depth of loyalty and my mindset. My father ignored her muddy statement and came near me to ask the whole matter. He knew I won't do anything which could make him cheerless, but the extras in the house were interrupting continuously making the whole matter a mere entertainment for them. They wanted me to move back to Sadri - the place where we came from. As usual, my father acted according to their will; otherwise, they would have banished him from their society. I wanted to tell my parents everything in actual form, but fate told them earlier in a very nasty way. If I would have told them everything clearly then too it would have been a sin to love someone. My parents were in grief. They surmised that their daughter betrayed them. I was crestfallen with their attitude.

The next morning itself, I was sent to Sadri with my relatives. My parents came to bid goodbye to everyone but I didn't look at them even once. I don't know what was their reaction when they saw me behaving in an uncouth manner. We reached Sadri after two hours of journey.

Our village house was big, with a lobby in the centre and surrounded by rooms. I saw baa, my grandfather, sitting on his wooden chair in front of his room. He was glaring at me, like I was a culprit. I walked near him and did salaam, but he was not interested in greeting me. So, I stepped back. My aunt called and showed me my room. It was a big but sparse room with only a bed and nothing else. I entered in, kept my bags and went to sleep.

The people staying in the house started training their eyes on me as if I was a woman who didn't hold any character. They were training me to live my life in affliction. The feeling of angst was strangling me like a vile creeper. I lost all hopes regarding my future with Ranil.

There was no source of amusement in that house. Gossiping about people was the only way they entertained themselves, and I was the latest buzzing topic.

One night I was looking at the sky, full of stars. Those stars were scintillating beautifully. At the same time my eyes glittered too, but with tears in it. "I am missing you Ranil!" I whispered. I knew, somewhere Ranil too was feeling that pain. I cried that whole night making the pillow wet.

Next morning, I was somewhere between deep sleep and waking up. The sunlight was not allowing me to sleep but I didn't want to open my eyes. I got out from my bed to close the curtains, but through the window, I saw some people gathering in the courtyard. I rubbed my eyes and goggled in bewilderment. Horror-struck, I rushed out. "What happened? Why are so many people present here?" I asked one of my aunts.

"Dear, you are going to be part of our gang" she chuckled answering me.

"What gang?" I was unable to grasp her intention behind those words.

"The gang of married ones, hahaha! Ruhani dear, such an innocent child you are! I don't know how you will handle your in-laws" she said pinching my cheeks.

Whatever she said was not amusing me. "I am not going to get into this fake and forceful relationship. I can't ruin my life simply out of fear. I was duped into thinking that I was guilty. Their honour will be celebrated for two days, but my entire life will be reduced to rubble" I murmured. I had been stunned; the aunt's statement had baffled me. I tried to imagine my future with Imran, my so-called fiancée, but the mere thought was enough to clobber my heart. The thought of getting apart from Ranil was scratching me deeply.

I asked for a mobile phone from one of my cousins and rang up my parents. After that, I called up Ranil. I told him to burn my memories and our dreams of togetherness. Ranil brushed aside my idea and got ready to confront Baa, the controller. Feeling agitated I countered his idea; it was a perilous act. But his optimism altered my outlook. I agreed with a hope that after meeting and knowing Ranil, the man would unequivocally welcome him. Perhaps, I was ambivalent regarding his presence.

*

Abandoning myself into desolation I woke up unwillingly to initiate my daily routine. I went out of my room to clean the veranda. Holding a big broom in my hand I was sweeping the neelgiri leaves with full attention, so as to not leave even a single leaf behind. 'Tang Tang' chimed the clock seven times, announcing that it was 7 O' clock. Once, 7:00 O' clock had a different meaning in my life. I was an independent girl living alone in capital city of state, rising and shining with an aim to spread smiles. But what was sense of providing emotional sensations when reality was cutting a rug remorselessly in front of me. In spite of that I repeated to myself to not despair, but my stars weren't working according to my will."

"You know Ruhani, you let your whole mind swing like a pendulum between the past and future. The mind plays tricks with us. Don't allow it to do so. Be aware and don't let the mind get drifted away by random thoughts" Anjali spoke, awakening her counsellor soul again.

However, Ruhani was not in the frame of mind to get any advice. With a deadpan expression, she looked at Anjali and continued, "It wasn't like that always. I was aware about the present moment and not everything happening to me was hair-raising. My fortune shone when I got a chance to see my parents making an entrance in the village house all of a sudden. Throwing the broom away, I ran fast to enfold them in my arms. Slipping into bliss, the three of us made a cocoon by embracing each other.

My mother's lips became a fountain of kisses. She looked at me with tears in her eyes. On the contrary my father had dry eyes. He was looking at me with love but I could also see the guilt in his eyes. Till now, our trio was silently conveying messages of endearment to each other.

"Give me this paa..." I said, taking the bags from my father's hand.

"How are your beta?" finally uttered my father, caressing my head. Unable to control myself I broke down, wailing and shouting to take me back to my happy land. Ceaselessly I kept complaining about every relative. I felt sure that looking at my condition my father would surely swing into action. Guess what? I was stupid enough to ask for something from people who were handcuffed!

"Now let them come inside. Cry later" Spoke my Badi Mummy from the kitchen where she was making millet bread.

Hearing her voice, my parents went inside to greet her. I was standing alone at the gate. Slowly lifting the bags, I walked towards my room. Abruptly I heard footsteps making heavy sound of boots. Taking one breath I turned back and was left goggling at the man with my mouth open!! I wondered, is this scene real or am I hallucinating? As soon as I came to my senses, I was elated to see the person who had entered. I was all set to run and embrace him, but thankfully, realising the barriers around me, I quickly controlled my senses.

Till then, all the members of the house gathered in the veranda glaring with him in hostility. Ranil was entering in at a languid pace. The handmade paintings and cow dung cakes were enthralling his eyes, but less than me. He was looking around the house to escape from the strange looks everyone was giving him. Then, he walked up to me and stood by my side in the courtyard where Baa was sitting on a small cot and rest of the people were standing around him.

We, as a couple, confronted Baa and revealed everything fearlessly. He was listening to us with full attention and was examining Ranil from head to toe. After hearing to our plea, he gave a totally unanticipated response. He smiled and adored me for being doughty. His words made me and my parents dive into sparkles. As Baa praised me in front of everyone, the bitterness on their faces became a treat to see!

Baa greeted Ranil tenderly. Overwhelmed on seeing that improbable view, I wiped my moist eyes. "Finally, I will be living with the man of my dreams" I mused. Ranil walked near to Baa and bowed to touch his feet. But all of a sudden, that man with a giant, fake nose attacked Ranil with his *lath* (stick)!! The sound of the *lath* banging onto Ranil's head was so loud that it shook me to the core!! I could see blood gushing out of Ranil's head. I felt as if half of my heart was lying vulnerable and helpless on the floor, under the wicked man's feet. I was traumatised watching the unwanted scene. "Ranilllll...!!!" I shouted with immense agony. "Somebody save him, please save him." I requested. I screamed, I yowled in agony, but ignoring me completely, each and every man in the house started thrashing Ranil. "Please leave him! Don't hit him!!" I begged everyone, but none of them paid heed to my pleas. After a while, I started spanking those reprobates. Seeing no effect on them, I picked up the broom and thrashed them using all energy I had.

My elder cousin who I was ceaselessly beating, shoved me and growled in his rasping voice - "Better for you to stay away. I won't think twice repeating this with you." But who cared? I jumped again and this time, was pulled aside by my father. Looking at him I joined my palms. Suddenly, he hugged me and started crying.

I knew he held no authority and the situation was going out of hand. I had to do something. Unclasping myself from his arms I ran towards Baa. Keeping my head on his feet, I cried, entreating him to show some mercy. But it was utterly idiotic of me to expect such precious emotions from him. Totally indulged into his ego, Baa sat relishing the catastrophe like it was a circus.

Ranil was being beaten harshly; my parents too cried for that innocent person. But those morons just knew the language of abhorrence? How could they understand my tender ones?

In the frenzy of wrath, this time I picked up a heavy stick and started drubbing all of them hard. Seeing my craziness for Ranil, my uncle grabbed my hair, and dragging me barbarously he hurled me in a room and locked it. I didn't know what they did with Ranil. Like every controversial love story, ours too faced this phase.

I was tremendously worried about Ranil. Was he ok? Did anyone help him? I kept cursing myself for being responsible for calling him here. Why did I allow him to come here to meet these barbarians who did not deserve his presence? I was on the edge as I wanted to know about his condition.

Anjali interrupted "Ohh... now I understood the reason behind your shouts that time. What happened later?"

"When news of my marriage reached people's ears, everyone in the village, in the clan, in the house, were exhilarated; except me. They all were ready to attend my wedding, but was it a wedding for me? No, it was like a suicide. 'I am not that great to commit an altruistic suicide. Even my God ordered me to choose the one who I like. Then what gave these people the right to overrule God's will? Why are they snatching my life? Everyone here has faced woeful situations in their life at some point, but why do they hold grudges against a person who wants to be happy? Why do they desire to always stuff others in the abode of the damned?' I thought helplessly. I had become meek and vulnerable that time."

"Hello Ruhani" came a voice. "Why these swollen eyes? You should look radiant. Come on, you are going to get married, you will see a whole new world now." The woman was my cousin sister 'Heena', the only one who I admired. Heena added. "Do you know, Ruhani? We women are bound to follow the rules which are made by these men for fulfilling their pleasures. But don't worry, the person who you are getting married to is a holy person. He performs all religious activities. He offers prayers five times a day and he is a graduate too – so, up to your level."

"No Heena, he is not. Does only performing religious activities make him good? What about his deeds? What about my will, my choice? Is it fine to marry someone forcefully? Open our religious book and show me where it is written. Heena, don't just follow what others told you. Open the book and read."

"Ruhani please, you were engaged to him when you were a mere teenager. You knew that someday you have to marry him. Then why did you have to rebel?"

"Heena, you can't understand. I haven't done anything intentionally. I can't do anything now. I can't marry Imran."

"Enough Ruhani! Now come with me, someone wants to meet you."

"Meet me!? No, I don't want to meet anyone." I said, but from within I hoped that she might be talking about Ranil.

"No excuses, come with me fast." Gripping my wrist forcefully, she took me on the terrace.

"Stand here. I will come in a few minutes." Saying this, she turned around and walked downstairs.

She left me alone with my thoughts alternating between horrifying ones thinking about my so-called fiancée's entry and joyous ones hoping for Ranil's arrival. Just then, I heard someone calling my name:

"Ruhani."

I turned back and saw a man coming near to me. I looked at him with a confused expression. Seeing that, he said,

"Oh, it seems you are unable to recognize me! Ok let me tell you; I am the one whom you are engaged with" the man spoke smirking at me.

"Imran!!!" I squealed, immediately getting enveloped in negative vibes.

"Listen Ruhani, I know everything about that boy. I don't know what happened between you both? Hope you understand what I mean by that? But in spite of that I am ready to marry you" said Imran, holding my hand.

"Shut up! What do you mean by saying 'what happened between me and him?' Do you think love only means getting intimate? Listen, you are not impelled to marry me. You don't need to show yourself as some benevolent person. I don't want to marry you, so leave me alone!" I spoke pouring out my anger and jerking his hand.

My act lacerated his masculine pride. Wounded and fumed, he yanked my hairs and growled, "What do you think of yourself, huh?! It's my greatness that I am getting married to a girl who has no reputation left among us. This is the result of educating girls. Education gifts them an impertinent attitude. Listen you big-head, you are not the queen of some estate. You just hold a Master's degree, and are swollen with pride on that teeny-weeny reason." Saying this he clasped my wrist. Twisting it painfully, he added - "Wait and watch what I am going to do after this marriage. Your egotistical nature will disappear at the soonest, I promise."

Saying this, he pushed me away and stomped off in a huff. I sat on my knees and started crying loudly, as if somewhere Ranil could my screech. "How can I marry a person who doesn't know the meaning of love?! Who doesn't know that a woman is a human being too, not a mere puppet!" I thought?

After a few minutes, Heena came upstairs. "So, what did he say?" she asked questioningly.

I removed my hands from my face, stood up, and gave her a tight slap!

"You were convincing me to marry this person? He, who doesn't know how to respect a woman?! Never! I can never agree to marry him!" I yelled at her.

"Listen Ruhani, love does bloom after marriage. His behaviour will change after you marry him, understood? And listen don't try ever to go against family norms...." she threatened me.

"Heena, I thought you are different, but I was mistaken. Good night." Pushing her away, I went downstairs to my room and did the thing which I was doing a lot those days - cry.

Chapter 10
The Tower of Dreams collapses

I was steadily looking at the dull wall, my mind wandering in the dark woods of negative thoughts. To ignore them, I turned my eyes towards a small jharokha (peeping window), and tried to see the hustle-bustle in the veranda. Soon, I saw Heena running towards my room with trembling steps.

"Ruhani, today's is your 'Mehendi ki raat'[1]. Please cooperate and won't create any drama." Saying this she turned around and walked straight towards my Bua.

How lightly she spoke those words? Little did she know that they fell like thunder on me. Sighing with a totally blank mind, I pulled my hair and went in search of a rope to attempt suicide.

It took me few minutes to bring myself back to my senses. Chewing over disparate ideas to rid of my present situation I finally planned to run away from

---

[1] A night where brides-to-be are applied henna to the accompaniment of joyous songs

that place when everyone would get occupied with merriment.

Coming near the door, I looked at the sunset twilight sky. I saw the sun gradually distancing itself. It seemed as if each of its red ray occupying the sky was alerting me for the upcoming ordeal. Not wasting even a single second, I set foot outside the room to analyse the situation. Ambling in the veranda I saw one of its corner occupied by cooks. They were the same cooks who had prepared appetizing dishes on my engagement day. The head cook was stirring dessert in giant utensil with a big ladle, unfurling fragrant aromas all around. In another corner, folk singers, who we call 'Langaas', were sitting crossed-legged on the carpet, as they unpacked their musical instruments. Baa sat in front of them on his comfort chair and demanded to listen "Chirmi mhari". The lead singer of the group started crooning the song, and was soon joined by other singers. Honestly saying, their ebullient performance could make even musical anhedonics groove on their rhythm.

Watching me roam in the house so freely, my aunt sent Heena with a command to make me sit on the cot which was placed in middle of veranda and get my face veiled. I looked at her with enmity; however, not throwing much tantrums, I obeyed her. On my left, some women were mixing water and myrtle powder for the function. Observing their extreme engagement in the activity I smirked. Poor ladies, they didn't have any idea that the girl sitting next to them was a rebel. They would not be getting a chance to colour her palms. I wasn't ready for the fate they all were deciding for me.

Hitherto I had seen every member of the family, except my parents. Their disappearance was proof of their agony. They were unable to see their daughter walking towards her burial chamber. However, at that moment, I cursed them for lacking hardihood to speak up for their only daughter. You know what? I still feel like slapping myself hard for spilling venom."

"Don't, dear. Do not live in regret. Your mind was overflowing with negative emotions at that time. You need to forgive yourself; you are not a bad person" Anjali's mild words mesmerized Ruhani. She spoke rarely, but when she spoke, she had that soothing voice which felt as if it was caressing one's mind. "So, what happened next?" Anjali added.

"Hmmm... Gradually guests started gathering in the house. Among them, some were relatives, some were strangers and some were acquaintances. In that crowd, one familiar face captivated my eyes. Through my chiffon dupatta I peered at that face, which had a well-grown beard and moustache. Taking a wall's support, he was standing beside the main gate. Gazing at me he beamed, and I instantly recognized him. It was Ranil!! 'Thank god he is fine, but why is he putting his life on stake again?' I thought. I had planned everything, and he would unintentionally ruin everything. 'I must tell him to leave' I thought. As soon as I got an opportunity, I sneaked behind the house, signalling Ranil to follow me without being noticed.

Reaching the isolated zone of the house, I gingerly touched his wounds and embraced him. "What are you doing here? Don't you know them? They all are wicked folks, run away. I can't let you suffer because of my selfishness." But Ranil was relaxed and calm as if he had planned everything well. He said- "Shut up Ruhani, what selfishness? You want me to leave you alone with these felons to slaughter you for the sake of preserving their honour?! Believe me, everything will be okay. I had lost all hopes when they separated us. I was in a state of nerves when I was discharged from the hospital and was continuously thinking about your condition. It's our final chance; no convincing anymore. Let us elope."

"Ranil, are you sure you want flee away? Trust me, I do have another plan. I will convince my parents and I know they will understand. I haven't yet got a chance to dispel their doubts. Have you disclosed our relationship in front of your parents?"

"Well, I lied to them. I still lack courage to tell them everything, but believe me, once we get together, everything will be fine."

"You should have told them everything." I shouted, not because I was still a secret for his parents, but due to actual anger was on his arrival.

"I didn't find it correct, but Rushil doubted and approached me, asking about the real matter. Till date, I had never shared anything with him, but for the first time I spoke my heart out. He suggested me to come here after few days along with some known men, but I found it right to come now. We don't have much time."

"Ranil! I told you to keep Rushil away from this matter."

"Ruhani, I know there are some differences between both of us, but after all he is my brother. He was ruffled by knowing the reality." Ranil spoke in one breath, without thinking that the news distressed me.

I was aghast to hear that. Even though Rushil was good, it was hard to trust him after the enmity we shared. I became suspicious about him because he possessed feelings of love for me. Why was he concerned about us? Various questions were revolving in my head, when suddenly Baa came to the place where we were talking. 'Did he know about Ranil's advent? Was he already clued up about everything? If yes, then who was the person behind it?' I don't know why, but my heart and mind were becoming dubious about Rushil's intentions behind fostering Ranil.

"Sorry to disturb you, lovebirds!" Baa spoke twirling his moustache.

At that time, I thought 'Why would have Rushil encouraged Ranil? I looked at Ranil and spoke – "Was this the pain healing therapy by the person who can never see us together?" I was incredulous about Rushil's good intentions.

This time me and Ranil both felt the pain of those bamboo sticks. I told Ranil to run away, but he kept on sharing the pain with me and endeavoured to rescue me. I clutched his hand and bolted through the backdoor. We ran and ran, till we suddenly noticed our feet having landed on concrete! Elated that we had hit the main road, we started running wherever the road was taking us. Eventually, a flash of light forced our eyes to close. In the next moment, we found ourselves lying on the bed of concrete and cement, with crimson red blood splattered all over it.

"What happened after that? How did he become your husband? Did everything become normal after that incident?" Anjali asked with some puzzlement in her mind.

"I remember, I was hospitalized. The police came to inquire about the accident, but my Baa's political influence restrained them from conducting their duty well.

"And what about Ranil? Haven't the police asked him anything?"

"I don't know about Ranil. He never speaks much about it. But that incident brought some moments of relaxation in my life. I got a respite from an undesirable wedding. My life was moving in a sluggish way, and so were my tears. I was taken back to those days when I always whimpered thinking about Ranil.

I was again moving into depression; my life had withered. Travelling to the past, recalling my struggles, and crying over my painful journey had become a habit. Anyone who will hear my story will surely shiver and thank God for his/her blessed life."

"Ruhani…" Anjali said holding Ruhani's hand. "You know, there are billions of people in this world, and everyone has their different story of pain. Don't take me otherwise, but you need to understand that this society moulds you according to their personality. In tandem with that, we have a reflective behaviour. We become what we see. In cinema, we see sad actors and actresses, who cry over lost love, and somehow live their life with that sadness. This affects us a lot. We see ourselves as great people who have exciting life stories of themselves to tell this world. Do that if you think it motivates people. But don't try to relive those stories again and again. You need to realise this." Looking at Anjali like a child, Ruhani tried to detangle her words. She was impressed by lady's deep thoughts again. Silently observing her she waited for her to speak again. "Well, did Ranil arrive after that?" Anjali asked.

"Yes, he kept his promise this time. One day while sitting on the terrace I felt as if the soft blowing wind was conveying a message to me. A message that 'all these hard days are going to fade away, my dedication for one person will not remain unrewarded'. In the same moment, I saw something out of the blue. I saw him once again. Slowly he came close to me. Looking at him, my eyes were filled with tears. Later, I started squalling. I was bemoaning the lack of sensibility my family had for not understanding our love. 'But how did he manage to come up? How did everyone in the house allow him to come on the terrace? Is there no one in the house? They must have gone somewhere....' I thought.

Ranil rubbed my head, wiped my tears and spoke - "Don't over think." I was shocked to listen this. Simply by looking at my facial expressions, he had easily grasped the restlessness I was experiencing. He hugged me tenderly.

For me, spending those harrowing days in a place from where I wanted to run off was like breathing in Gehenna[2]. My soul was deceased; thankfully just his one hug revitalised me. After calming me down, Ranil requested me to come with him. But I denied. I was not in the condition to see him again going through the same suffering. He clutched my hand and started walking downstairs. Reaching the courtyard, I don't know from where I gained boldness to call out to everyone loudly. Hearing my roar, each and every one rushed out from their rooms. The good thing was that except my father and Baa,

---

[2.] **Gehenna** or Gehinnom (literally translated as "Valley of Hinnom") is thought to be a small valley in Jerusalem. In the Hebrew Bible, **Gehenna** was initially where some of the kings of Judah sacrificed their children by fire. Thereafter, it was deemed to be cursed (Book of Jeremiah 7:31, 19:2–6).

rest of the men were out of the house. Ranil and I were standing in front of them, holding each other's hand. My relatives glowered at us. Without waiting for them to speak anything I started throwing my words at them - "Listen everyone, enough is enough. I will not tolerate this anymore. It is better that you allow me to go with Ranil with your blessings."

"Are you fine dear?" Asked my parents looking at me in a strange way. My mother came running near me and urged to lower my pitch.

Abruptly my aunt opened her dirty mouth and vomited - "Ruhani, have you lost your mind? What are you saying? Tie your tongue and march straight to your room."

"Well, I don't think I am someone's personal property. Tell me if I am doing despicable crime. I want to marry a person with who I want to spend the rest of my life, that's it. You all are misled by fallacious beliefs of this society. Do you know what kind of wickedness you have in this so-called reputed society of yours? Extra-marital affairs, disloyal nature, characterless men and women... and you are questioning my love?" I replied. Ranil was standing quietly, displaying beaming at me to show his support. His serene aura gave me the strength to face everyone present there.

Abruptly, Baa's roar sounded from behind me - – "Let her go, no one will stop her ...she has lost her mind. Bloody black spot on my family! Let her go. Shoo girl... shoo" he bellowed like a demon.

The only people in agony were my parents. They looked at me helplessly. I hugged my mother in a way like I was never going to see her again. She was yowling in pain - the pain of being unable to speak anything in her daughter's support. I looked at my father and wanted him to caress me, but he didn't show any kind of action which could have made me feel secure. Leaving my parents was an agonising moment for me, but I didn't have any option. They didn't have the courage to speak in favour of their only daughter, and I didn't want to live my life in the jaws of death.

I packed my bags; my mother helped me with some money. She asked 'why am I behaving insane?' But I didn't reply to her. Slowly reversing my steps, I moved ahead with Ranil towards the exit. Everyone's eyebrows were shrunk in fury, but I was feeling free from chains. Albeit I was not leaving that house with contentedness. I had always dreamt leaving my paternal home as the happiest bride ever; unluckily, that didn't happen.

"But why did Baa allow you to leave so easily?" Anjali asked in confoundment.

"May be because everyone in the village now knew about his grand-daughter's shameless act? What else could be the reason?" spoke Ruhani with her eyes steady on a painting of Caucasian woman carrying fruit in a basket.

@

Holding Ruhani's hand, Anjali was walking along with her towards the washroom.

"You are a very caring person" Ruhani remarked. After a few minutes she came out. Taking support of the wall beside her, she slowly trudged towards her bed. Noticing her, Anjali quickly came forward to give her a hand. "How are you feeling now?" she asked.

"Better."

Sitting beside Ruhani, Anjali took a tablet from a small box and asked, "So, where did Ranil take you after you left your home?"

"He took me to a posh apartment, where had he purchased flat for us. He had mentioned this thing when we had met in Jaipur. It was a flourished township with different apartments. Our building read 'Sukoon Apartments'. It was a giant building, with a 60-foot-tall main gate. Every building seemed to be of 12 storeys, painted in metallic grey. We entered the building. All of a sudden, Ranil recalled that he had an urgent work to do in the office. He told me to meet the secretary of the apartment and collect the keys from him. I agreed because Mr Das knew about me and Ranil. I walked to the watchman and asked him to call the secretary. He looked at me from head to toe and rang the secretary. After a few minutes, I saw Mr Das coming with a broad smile on his face. He had a very pleasant personality.

"Hello Mrs Ruhani." He greeted me pleasantly. Arghh! Awkward moment! But all the same, it was soothing to hear being called 'Mrs. Ruhani'.

"Do you know me?" I asked.

"Yes, I know you. Around 2-3 months ago, Ranil told me that he is going to marry you. He also showed your picture to our family. Were you not supposed to be here earlier? You have been delayed by almost a month."

"Yes sir, but something went wrong with us. Unluckily we met with an accident."

"Oh! So sorry. I didn't know that. Actually, we were enjoying vacations out of India for almost a month. Where is Ranil?"

"He left for his office for confronting some urgent issues."

"Oh...Okay. I will meet him later then. Take these keys."

"Thank you very much, Mr Das."

Having this small conversation, I moved inside the elevator and pressed the button for the 10th floor. As the elevator reached our floor, I stepped out and started searching for our flat. I stopped at a wooden coloured door which had a name-plate showing our names 'Mrs. Ruhani and Mr. Ranil." I was very happy! After a long period, my dream had finally manifested into reality. It proved that patience actually gives results.

"Ruhani… wait... wait for me" shouted Ranil. I was shocked to see him but was happy as well.

"Hey! You came so early."

"I was on the way, but the matter was resolved. Well, Mr Das was praising you."

"You met him!"

"Yes, he was standing at the entrance gate of the building. Leave that. So, are you ready to step into your new world?" he asked bowing down.

I nodded my head and felt my heart beating wildly. As soon as I opened the main door, it felt as if my eyes were seeing paradise on earth. The walls of our flat were shimmering phenomenally. The golden colour on the main wall was so alluring. Large-sized photos of Ranil and me from our schooldays were hung on the wall. My eyes rolled over the well-furnished house, the sofas, the tables, and rest of the furniture. There was a small pool-like structure in the centre of the hall. It had pink coloured water, and different kinds of flowers and small candles were floating over it. The balcony's boundary was covered by the rose plants. Each rose was red and fresh, the air blowing in the balcony was touching the roses and wafting its sweet fragrance to every corner of our home. Ranil had made all the arrangements just for me. It was inconceivable. I was dancing in my own rhythm and Ranil was looking at me gaily. I was teasing him, laughing with him, dancing with him! We both looked into each other's eyes. His eyes were so deep, so pure, so soothing! My heart felt light as a feather just gazing into them. But then, all of a sudden, a dark cloud descended on my mind. I was gripped by an unknown fear! A fear that someone will snatch Ranil from me. A fat tear rolled down from my eye. Ranil wiped it out and said - "Ruhani don't cry. Promise me, this will be your last tear. I want your smile to be so cheap so that I could have it every time I see you but your tears should be precious, very precious" he whispered. I felt fortunate to have man like Ranil beside me. Suddenly he started singing -

"Mili mujhko jannat toh jannat ke badle

Khuda se meri jaan tumhein maang lega

Mera pyaar wo hai ke, marke bhi tumko

juda apni baahon se hone na dega."

I gazed at him and spoke- "Why is this song so close to your heart? You always sing this for me when you finish saying something poignant."

"That's because each and every of its line belongs to you. I love listening to old songs. They are so melodious and meaningful."

"Your brother is totally opposite to you. He loves ear splitting music" I replied and kissed Ranil on the lips. He twisted his tongue in amazement and continued, "Ruhani, I love you." For me, the power of those words was inestimable. I thanked god for eliminating all the dark forces from my life.

Ranil and I had beatific expressions on our faces, experiencing the blessings of God upon us. We were creating magical moments together. We became so busy in adoring each other that it didn't allowed my past to horrify me. In spite of many flaws, we considered ourselves perfect."

"Okay... what about the surrounding? Your neighbours?" asked Anjali tilting her head.

"Aaaa... our neighbours.... they were amiable, but I think they were not happy with Ranil. They ignored him a lot. There were no greetings or welcome for him from their side. I saw them getting annoyed whenever I introduced him to them. "Had he done something wrong? If yes, then what?" I would ruminate often. Ranil told me not to over think; if they ignored him, it was out of jealousy, and nothing else.

Two days passed swiftly. We were living our life peacefully, but on the third day when Ranil was not present in the house, some people knocked the door. I opened it to see some women and two men wearing a white dress coming inside. They requested me to come with them. I denied, but they forced me. Clasping my hand, one of the women started pulling me. "How dare you hold my hand like this?!" I thundered, shocked at their illicit behaviour, but they were quiet. They brought me to the ground floor of the apartment. I pleaded everyone standing there to help me. Mr Das gave me vexed look and ignored me. I cried and tried my best to remove their hands but it was a futile attempt. Finally, they made me sit in a van, which read 'Gayatri Mental Hospital'! I was taken to the hospital. I kept screaming Ranil's name continuously, but he was nowhere on the scene. 'Where has he gone?! Who is responsible for all this? Are my relatives trying to keep us apart, or, is it Rushil?' I kept thinking constantly on a loop. I was so exhausted thinking about Ranil's disappearance that my overused brain made me slumber. When I woke up, I saw a person in a white coat standing before me. I rubbed my eyes to see him properly and then said - "I am alright. Please let me go. I am living peaceful life with my husband." For once, the doctor stared at me like I spoke something wrong, but without replying to any of my questions, he moved on leaving me hopeless.

"Where should I go now? Where is Ranil? Why is he not here? Where is he stuck now?" I kept thinking.

Days passed on, but Ranil did not come to discharge me from the hospital, where each and every day was tormenting me. I was waiting for him to take me back to the life which he had gifted me; where we were together. At last, I lost all hopes. 'He won't come, Ruhani' I spoke to myself, crying rivers. 'Is he gone again? Why is he not here? What does he want from his life now? Is he gone again to grab what he wants? You should hate him. He left you in this situation all alone. No, why am I thinking like this? I should not.' My internal voices were busy arguing with each other and I was sitting soundlessly, all alone in a ward.

"So, did Ranil come back?"— Anjali questioned breaking her long silence.

"Huh…. no…." said Ruhani with intensity in her eyes.

"So how did you reach in that area? I mean, the place where accident took place?" Anjali asked incredulously.

"Well, I am unable to recall anything clearly. I spent the last few days in that mental hospital mostly in an un-conscious state. Yes, doctor did test me and declare that I was okay. He apologised for the mistake too."

"Ok ok … now you should take rest. Don't take load" said Anjali caressing Ruhani's hair.

Ruhani looked at Anjali and glittered.

Anjali came out from the room and saw Mr Singh approaching her.

"Is she alright to make the statement? Did she tell you anything?"

"Yes, probably everything, but she is unable to recall the past few days of her life or the days which she spent in a mental hospital."

"Mental hospital! But why?" asked Mr Singh.

"Long story behind it, sir. The purpose of admitting her in a mental hospital is still unknown."

Anjali and Mr Singh became busy analysing the facts but they were interrupted by the heavy voice of a lady - 'Mrs Barkha' - a woman in her 50s, with her face painted with heavy makeup, and her body adorned with gold jewellery. Her over-the-top appearance was hurting everyone's eyes present there.

"Hello Inspector Abhimanyu Singh, how are you dear?"

"Oh, hello aunty, I am fine."

"Well, I know we are not such close relatives but sometimes you should come to our place to meet us" said Mrs Barkha in a taunting manner

"Of course, aunty, I shall come sometime soon. I have been posted here only recently. But for now, I am busy solving some cases" humbly answered the cop.

"Okay, so are you here to solve a case?" asked the lady, and tried to peep inside the room through the small glass window. Mrs Barkha looked at the lady sleeping beautifully. She exclaimed- "She is Ruhani! How come she is here?!"

"Do you know her?" in the Inspector and Anjali both remarked eagerly, hoping for a possible breakthrough in the mysterious case.

"Yes. She is my neighbour. She lives in the same apartment as mine. Few days ago, she was sent to the mental hospital. We wanted her to leave the building. We were all frightened with her behaviour. Barmy she is!"

"But what had she done? Why were you all scared of her behaviour?"

Mrs Barkha answered — "Because she used to talk to herself all alone! She introduced us to her husband who was invisible or never existed."

"What?! Invisible!" exclaimed Anjali in abject horror. "What are you saying?"

"Yes dear, that's why we sent her to the hospital. I don't know much about the owner of the house, but the flat in which she lives was purchased by Mr Daga's son. Our secretary tried to contact them but he couldn't. He told us that the Daga family was not in the city. We didn't have much time. There were chances that her condition could get worse with time. Everyone was of the opinion that it was best to send her to the mental hospital. I think she must have run away from that place. I never knew she is here. But it's good. Keep this curse with you till possible or better still, send her back to the mental hospital."

"Mrs Barkha, have you ever heard of human rights commission?" Anjali asked indignantly.

"No, what is that?" replied Mrs Barkha, believing Anjali to be speaking in her support.

"Wow, you haven't heard of it yet? If you knew about it, you, your secretary and those morons of your society wouldn't have dared to do such an inhuman act with this innocent lady."

"Everything was done for sake of the lady's welfare, okay?!" the woman said in a shivering voice. "Ok then, I have to go now take care." Saying so, the hypocritical woman made a hasty exit.

"But she said Ranil was with her!" Exclaimed Anjali. "She told me the entire conversation which they had between them. Then why did Mrs Barkha say such mean things? Oh, my God, I am so confused" Anjali exhaled, suddenly feeling very drained out.

"I need to know about this Ranil and the owner of the flat. Ask this lady about Ranil's permanent address...." Mr Singh murmured.

Chapter 11
The upcoming enigma

Mr Singh drove off to Mr Daga's house. The entry had a big name-plate which read - 'Rajeev Daga'. Mr Singh read the name and approached the watchman who informed his master about Mr Daga. Mr Singh then crossed the gate and saw the house which was built marvellously. A well-maintained garden surrounded the triangular-shape house. The garden contained small lotus type structures, which were actually small rooms. The main door was made up of glass and showed greenery inside the house. A white-bearded person wearing a cream-coloured kurta-pyjama opened the door for Mr Singh and requested him to be seated. Mr Singh started looking around the large room. One of the walls had an aquarium attached to it. Statues of lord Buddha and other beautifully carved marble structures were giving relief to his eyes. After few minutes, Mr Daga entered the room. Mr Singh stood up and spoke, "Hello sir, this is inspector Abhimanyu Singh."

"Hello inspector. So, what is the reason behind your presence in my house?"

"Sir, actually I wanted to know about your flat in Sukoon Apartments."

"What do you want to know about that flat and exactly which flat? I can't recall it."

"Actually sir, the flat was purchased by your son."

"Oh yes I remember. My son told me once, but I haven't paid much attention to it. So, what do you want to know about that?"

"Sir, a girl named Ruhani was living there with her husband."

"What?" Mr Daga interrupted. "How could she? Whoever she is, she is living in my son's flat illegally. Throw her stuff out of the flat."

"Yes sir, definitely, but I want to ask you a question. May I know something about your son?" asked Mr Singh.

"Well, I love my son a lot. It is commendable that in such a young age he established a huge business of his own. Not a single property of mine is under his name. I am a proud father of a brilliant son."

"Oh... that's great. Well, I want to ask him something on the matter of this case I'm behind. Can you call him, please?"

"I can't..." Mr Daga replied in a cracked voice, his eyes suddenly wet.

"Oh, has he gone somewhere? No problem. I can come later."

"No officer.........he is no more!" said a father with a shivering voice. "It's hard for me to even speak these words."

"Oh, I am extremely sorry! But, can you tell how it happened?" Mr Singh asked, keeping his tone soft and low.

"My son was an introvert, he never shared anything with us. Why he went to that place, we don't know. He met with an accident near a village more than a month ago. A girl too got injured in that accident. Both were taken to the hospital. That girl suffered a few injuries but my son lost his life on the way. People who took them to the hospital said that the girl's family came and took her immediately after. She was given first aid. Police told me that they inquired everything from her but she doesn't remember much. The police are trying hard. Let's see who the culprits are?"

"Hmm... I see." Trying to understand the case, replied Mr Singh.

"Oh... Inspector, here is Rushil - my younger son" suddenly Mr Daga said, looking at the boy entering in the room. Mr Singh nodded his head to greet him, as did Rushil. "Rushil, tell Abdul chacha to prepare tea for two. So, inspector, who is the girl living in that flat?"

"Sir, her name is Ruhani. She has been admitted to Kalyani hospital for some reason. Till now I only have this much knowledge" answered Mr Singh.

"Okay, okay."

Rushil was alarmed listening to Mr Singh and left the room.

"I am so sorry sir, but may I know the name of your son?" asked Mr Singh

"Yes, why not? His name was Ranil .... Ranil Daga." The proud father's eyes again became wet with tears.

Mr Singh stood up in utter shock! "What?! Ranil?"

"Yes Ranil. Why? What happened to you?"

"No... Nothing sir... umm, thank you..." Mr. Singh stammered, realising that it was the same name Riuhani had mentioned.

Abhimanyu Singh was totally confused now. "Is Ruhani really a mental case? That man died a month ago. Then, how could he be living with her?" Mr Singh's head was getting dizzy with all these thoughts. Somehow, he bade goodbye to Mr Daga and headed to his jeep.

From there, he drove off to Sukoon Apartments and met Mr Das.

"Yes, Ruhani had come to live here. I found her good when she met me for the first time. But then, she started behaving in an insane manner and soon after, I got the news of Ranil's death. I called at Mr Daga's house but didn't get a chance to talk to him on this matter because the whole family was out of state. Though Ranil had showed me her picture once but I don't think she was married to him. Her motive behind coming here is still an enigma. Was she fraud or mad? I don't know. But her mysterious nature horrified all of us. I didn't want to send her to the mental hospital. Many a times, I tried to ask her about her family to inform them about her condition, but every time she had only one answer 'I don't have anyone in this world except Ranil.' She was so confident speaking that lie. It never permitted me to doubt her. When I got to know about Ranil's death on the next day of her arrival, I wanted to tell her that he is not in this world. But I didn't want to create a mess. Hence, instead of filing a police complaint, I found a mental hospital to be a better place for her."

"Huhh... Ok, thank you Mr Das" said Mr Singh unable to deduct anything from Mr Das's words.

Abhimanyu Singh reached the hospital and asked for Ruhani. The woman was having forty winks. Her sleeping posture reflected as if she was dreaming about something which she always desires for.

"Hello sir, did you find anything?" Anjali asked on seeing Mr Singh.

"Hmmm, something really strange. Ranil Daga, the one who she called her husband, died more than a month ago. He does not exist now. I think this lady is going through some kind of mental illness" assumed the cop.

"I don't think so." Quickly spoke Anjali. "She is perfectly fine. I have talked to her extensively."

"Maybe she is telling a lie, but what about the behaviour which her neighbours noted? Why will she do this intentionally and make things more difficult for herself?" mused Mr Singh.

"This is really confusing sir..." said Anjali, clutching her forehead.

"Huhh… don't worry, let her wake up. We won't leave her like that. Call me when she is awake."

"Yes sir, sure."

Silence surrounded the scene. On the other side at Daga's mansion, Rushil was in a haste to go somewhere. He got dressed in his room, looked in the mirror, combed his hair and went off.

'Chhrrrrrrr….' A Car stopped in front of Kalyani Hospital. Rushil entered and asked the receptionist about the girl. She nodded her head and showed him the way.

He reached in front of the room and saw the lady in repose. Laying on the bed, Ruhani was looking like a fairy. He opened the glass door of general ward, and collided with Anjali. Looking at him sceptically, she asked his name.

"My name is Rushil, I am here to see Ruhani."

"Well, she is asleep. You have to wait till she wakes up." Anjali said with professional ease, hiding the feelings of surprise she felt.

"Can I just see her once?"

"Okay, come with me."

Rushil followed her quietly.

"Ruhani...." Uttered Rushil. Ruhani struggled to open her eyes and saw the blurred image of Rushil in front of her. Abruptly, Anjali rubbed her head and brought her back to the state of repose. Shutting her eyes, Ruhani drifted back to sleep.

"She needs rest. I told you to wait till she woke up."

"Okay, understood. I will wait outside" said Rushil. Both of them walked out.

"Sir you know her, so probably you can help the police in the investigation of this case. Let me call Mr Singh." Anjali tried Mr Singh's phone number but he was busy on another call. She told Rushil to sit on a bench and started searching for the cop in the hospital.

Finding it the best opportunity, Rushil returned to the ward and silently opened the door. Ruhani was back to the land of living. Tying her hair, she looked at Rushil.

"Hello Ruhani..." He greeted winking at her.

"Rushil!!! Why have you come here? How did you get to know about me? Tell me where is your brother? Has he gone somewhere to be more successful? Tell him that I need him, not these material things...." shouted Ruhani with wet eyes.

"For sure, but for that, you have to kill me first."

"Kill you?! For what?" Ruhani questioned agitatedly.

"Yes, kill me; because, he is no more. I have lost my brother; you have lost your love. I know he cared for you a lot, but now he is not in this world. How can you live your life like this?" Rushil spoke in a caring way holding Ruhani's hand.

Getting out from the bed Ruhani roared - "First of all Rushil, Ranil is alive. He took me from my home in front of my family. We were living together in our flat and were very happy. So go and tell your stories to someone else."

"Ruhani, you will be alright. I came here for you; I am there for you always." whispered Rushil and came near Ruhani to embrace her.

"No….no…. get away from me. Just go."

"Listen Ruhani, I know Ranil was a person who can never be forgotten. Even I found it difficult to accept the news of his death. I was totally devastated Ruhani, I had lost my brother!"

"No Rushil, he is alive. He was living with me. Your words are forcing me to doubt your intentions. You are evil. You control spirits, isn't it?"

"Are you mad? Who told you such trashy things about me?" Rushil thundered, gripping Ruhani's wrist.

"Ruby, your ex-girlfriend." Ruhani shouted, glaring at Rushil with bloodshot eyes.

Without paying attention to Ruhani's words, Rushil continued to convince her about Ranil's death, but she kept giving proofs of him being alive. Rushil's tolerance started wearing thin. His forehead shrivelled in fury. It was becoming difficult for him to resist his anger. Finally, he shouted,

"Listen Ruhani, Ranil is no more! How can he still be alive after that jeep banged him with such a great speed? How?"

Hearing that, Ruhani crinkled her eyes suspiciously and asked,

"How do you know it was a jeep?"

Rushil stammered and replied,

"Aaaa... someone...... told me...." But even as he said this, he stood stunned, his face grew pale. He sensed that he could not conceal the truth from Ruhani anymore now.

"Rushil, not a single person knew that it was a jeep. That means you are the one who was responsible for our accident!! You wanted to kill Ranil but unfortunately, I too met with that unlucky incident. How could you to this to your own brother? I hate you Rushil, I hate you. Bring my Ranil back, bring him back now...." the woman shouted with all her might.

"Who told you I was the only one responsible for this act? Your Baa, your so-called best friend Rohit..."

"Rohit?? How do you know him." asked Ruhani.

"Well, I got to know him after coming to this city. Ranil was his friend but alas... now he is no more" Rushil smirked.

"But why Rohit? He was Ranil's good friend" asked Ruhani standing stunned.

"Haha... the murderer is always ready to help another. They become best friends. A different kind of connection got built between them" said Rushil, mocking Ruhani.

"Murderer? Who else did he kill?"

"Your one and only, Dr Ozil. I got to know about this when Rohit was highly drunk one day. He had some personal issues with Ozil – perhaps, monetary matters. Rohit said it was an accidental death. Whatever it was, Rohit helped me a lot, otherwise his secret would have gotten revealed by me. Anyways, what do you have to do with them? Ozil is gone, and...and Ranil is also no more. Why are you destroying your life for them when they don't exist now?" Rushil spoke without having any expression of regret on his face. His brazenness had no limits!

Ruhani's eyes turned red. She gave him an odious look and roared, "How could you do this to your brother... howww?"

"Brother? No ways! He was my enemy. He snatched everything from me... everything that was destined for me. He was a thief, a scoundrel, he was never my brother. Never!!" Rushil shouted back without caring that the other patients were staring at them.

"No Rushil, Ranil always thought for you first. Every single time! And you? What did you do?! You killed my love! You are not a human.... Ruby was right!" Ruhani yelled grabbing the collar of Rushil's shirt.

Suddenly, she heard someone callout to her.

"Ruhani...."

"Ranilll......." she cried, as soon as she saw who it was, and ran towards him. Taking him in her arms like a whirlwind, she started kissing him everywhere on his face. After a while she turned and spoke - "See here, Rushil! Ranil is with me standing by my side. Now, do you have anything to say?! Hmm?" Then, she looked back at Ranil and said - "Do you know, this Rushil lied to me that you are no more. He made me cry so much. He is an evil person. He is not your brother! Now please discharge me from this hospital and let us go back to our home."

"Ruhani…" Breaking his silence Rushil spoke- "Do you think he is alive? Look at him carefully, can you feel the blood in his veins or hear his heartbeat? He is just a spirit, a hollow spirit, who I captured few days ago."

Ruhani roughly glared at Rushil and ignored his words. She looked deep into Ranil's eyes. Ranil was still but his eyes were uncovering his reality. Ranil's silence was the proof of his non-existence in this world. The sea of Ranil's deep eyes engulfed her. His continual gaze was making her travel her whole journey with Ranil. With a broken heart, Ruhani slowly walked in reverse. The desire for spending her whole life with her beau was curtailed but she was not ready to accept the truth. Taking her steps back continuously looking at Ranil, her head became heavy and her heartbeats became uncontrollable. As dizziness assailed her, she started stumbling while walking with leaden steps in the reverse direction. Rushil sprinted towards her and embraced to protect her from falling on the ground.

"Doctor, nurse…." Shouted Rushil. "Please come, see what has happened to her?" He was standing holding Ruhani, whimpering looking at her condition.

"Next time if you fall for someone…don't keep the Finagle Factor as an option…." Ruhani uttered sotto voce, closing her eyes.

Anjali and Dr. Sinha entered the room. "What just happened here?" Anjali asked in bafflement. The doctor inspected Ruhani and found that the body was in need of oxygen. She was immediately rushed to the emergency unit.

Beep beep beep……. the sound continued. Ruhani was on the hospital bed taking long breaths. Initially she struggled to inhale and exhale, but after some time, her condition returned to normal. The staff was relaxed to see the lady coming back to normal condition. Rushil was perturbed by the thought of losing his love. He was waiting for the doctors to come out and inform him about Ruhani's condition.

"Ok now, nurse, I think she is stable now" said Dr Sinha.

'Beeeeeeep……' All of a sudden came a long sound signalling the instability of patient's heartbeats!! "What is this? She was absolutely fine till now." Everyone present there were stunned to see sudden change in situation; the staff surrounded Ruhani again. Outside the emergency unit, Rushil's heart became restless. He started banging on the door to allow him to come inside. For Ruhani, the voices of the people surrounding her sounded like everything was in slow motion. Suddenly the flashback of her life was in front of her eyes. She saw a young Ruhani twinkling, dancing and chortling in keeping with her ebullient personality. She recalled the happy times which she had shared with her parents. She recalled the laughs shared with her friends. She recalled the hilarious moments spent with Shirley. At last, she recalled the moments spent with Ranil which she loved to reminisce every time. She mused on Ranil's promise - "These tears will be your last tears." Her eyes were filled with heavy tears that streamed down from both the sides of her face. The seven minutes of her life's flashback shackled the memories of the pain she went through. They showed Ruhani only the happiest moments of her life.

"Maybe there is another world, where I would meet you Ranil.... a world where love is not besmirched with the name of lust, where love is not connected with the honour of family. We will be together Ranil.... I promise you." Thinking this she slowly closed her eyes allowing her soul to fly high, away from this world.

Up in the seventh sky of god....

I love these kinds of beautiful and lovely people. Angels, I order to protect all those who live in the shade of love. Such kind of people are endangered nowadays.

"Hey Ruhani, are you awake? Are you able to make a statement now?" asked Anjali smiling at the lady. Slowly opening her eyes, Ruhani glanced around the ward.

"Oh! Am I alive!? Was I dreaming? Where is Ranil?" asked Ruhani scratching her head in perplexity.

"Keep calm, Ruhani."

"Yes, I am fine, tell me where is Ranil? she asked innocently.

"Actually Ruhani...." Anjali stammered with a grim expression on her face.

"Please nurse, don't push me into a maze of assumptions. Let everything be crystal clear" Ruhani pleaded.

Anjali looked at Mr Singh and swallowed nervously. Mr. Singh came forward and spoke, "Miss, Ranil is no more. He was dead when you both met with an accident." Ruhani convulsed with laughter listening to the information.

"Are you serious? Tell me this is a joke!" she said, and then suddenly, in the next moment, her yowl broke the stillness of the area. She was inconsolable. Crying her eyes out for an hour, she quietly covered herself with a blanket. Anjali came closer and removed the blanket from her face.

"Ruhani dear, be strong…" Caressing her hair, Anjali tried consoling her.

"I am sure Rushil murdered him. He confessed to me." Ruhani bleated.

"When?" asked Mr Singh.

"Few moments before he entered in and revealed the entire thing Ruhani answered wiping her tears.

"Ruhani, you were sleeping. I think you saw all this in your dream…." Anjali uttered offering her glass of water.

"But Rushil did come to see me."

"Yes, he did; but you were drowsy, so I haven't allowed him to meet you."

"What? Didn't he enter in without your permission?"

"Nothing like that happened. He is still waiting outside."

"What? God... it was a nasty dream, but if Rushil is not guilty then you are mistaken about Ranil's death. I was living with him in his flat."

"Miss, maybe it was your illusion. The man you are mentioning is dead!" Mr Singh stated emphatically.

"Oh! No, it's not possible. Ask Rushil about it. Rohit killed Ozil, maybe because of some monetary matter. Ozil had deep pockets... maybe Rohit was envious of his property."

"Hmmm, I came here after gathering all information. Rohit was involved in the murder of the doctor." Mr Singh said in a heavy voice.

"Yes Ruhani, Abhimanyu is right. He didn't know about the case. He has been posted to this city only recently" said Anjali.

"I don't believe this! Ranil is alive. I am fed up of repeating that we both were together in that flat. Please trust me!" pleaded Ruhani.

"Miss, you are repeating the same thing. Your neighbours, the people living in the apartment, never saw anyone residing with you. He wasn't there, he is dead."

"No, don't throw these false statements at me. Call Rushil" argued Ruhani being vexed. Getting out of the bed, she ran out to meet Rushil. Silently waiting for so long Rushil stood up in shock seeing his fragile best friend. Walking at a slow pace Ruhani came closer to him, snivelling. Quietly looking at each other they spoke some unspoken words.

$

Two months later....

"Hey Ruhani, wait for me" called Shirley following Ruhani.

"So, what did professor tell you?" Ruhani asked keeping her hand on Shirley's shoulder.

"Oh! He speaks a lot, but I haven't heard much. Hehehe...."

"Wow, that's how you are going to complete your PhD? Frankly speaking, you don't need it now."

"Haww!... Obviously, I need it. It's part of my interest. You got that, soon to be Dr as well as Mrs Ruhani?!" Shirley teased her best friend.

"You are still mad, Shirley."

"And always will be. Look, there is your soon-to-be husband" said Shirley pointing at a silver-coloured sedan.

"Yeah...exactly on time. Shirley, come with us. He wants to congratulate you."

"Hehe, tell him I have to still clear the interview."

"Don't worry, I know you will. Well, it was my dream to become a civil servant but you achieved that, hehehe. Come now, don't be stubborn." Ruhani said firmly.

"Nope, you guys enjoy your pre-wedding days, my *dhanno* is parked there. Bye bye!" waved Shirley as she walked away to her vehicle. Ruhani was looking at her with amazement. From all those past years her best friend's image was not less than that of a joker. In spite of that, the lady always walked with confidence, no co-dependency, no drama. She structured her life with bricks of light humour, love for herself and not draining her energy on worthy matters. Continuously gazing at her friend, Ruhani slowly walked towards the car and sat inside. Her fiancée drove the car to his new flat.

Sipping coffee Ruhani spoke, "That's strange, how could someone lie to be in a lost person's life again? I mean, though Rohit was his friend but Dr Ozil was never his friend. What was need of impressing me by saying he sent Dr Ozil to me?"

"Hmm... Ruhani, don't mull over these thoughts."

"Yeah... I know. But why did he come back in my life? Why?"

"That's because not everyone is strong. His girlfriend broke up with him before he came to you. Maybe his suffering pulled him towards you. Also, he said that you waited for him for so long without any selfishness involved. He was not at all in peace without you and he didn't find the same bond with the girl he met later. I think, with time he realised 'what he actually wanted?'. Though his words were bitter for me, I was bearing those words somehow as I didn't have any other option except helping him, and he knew that. He apologised to me for that. However, his sympathies were seeming to me like a taunt."

"Hmm... he must have shared these words when he visited my village for the last time."

"Yes, that day when I told him to act with patience, but he rushed and ruined everything."

"But what about those two days? My family says that when I left the house no one was accompanying me. I was alone, that is the reason my Baa and aunt called me barmy. But why do I feel like I spent those two days with Ranil in his flat. It wasn't my illusion."

"Don't think about it anymore. Everything is in the past now. Was it a visual hallucination? A dream? Leave everything behind now" said the loving fiancée who never resisted his beloved of discussing on the topic which had been already discussed for so many times.

"Or a spirit?" whispered Ruhani. Her fiancée grew pale. With wide open eyes he spoke - "That's all rubbish! I told you to do pranayama regularly. Are you doing that?"

"I will...God.... my life is no less than a drama" whispered Ruhani adjusting her engagement ring.

"Baby, it is all God's plan. Don't doubt it. All excruciating days have faded away. Relish your present with me. You know, what Kung-fu Panda taught us, right?"

"No way, not now!" uttered Ruhani with a fake cry.

"Okay then, come fast! I want to give a tight hug to my soon-to-be Mrs."

Ruhani sprinted towards her fiancée. Joyously taking her in his arms, he crooned,

"Mera pyaar wo hai ke

markar bhi tumko

juda apni baahon se

hone naa dega"

On hearing the song, she looked at her fiancée dumbstruck and asked, "Why did you sing this song?"

"Because I am dedicating this song for my ladylove" softly spoke Ruhani's man.

"You never liked old Hindi songs. You never dedicated such kinds of song for me. I know your taste in music."

"Ruhani, come on, it is just a song. What's the big deal?" spoke Rushil grinning and lifting Ruhani up to lay her on the bed.

"Tell me, who are you?" Ruhani whispered, looking at Rushil suspiciously.

"Your eternal love…" He answered looking deep into Ruhani's eyes, and winked at her as he gripped her wrists!